LUTHER
A Reformer for
the Churches

LUTHER
A Reformer for the Churches

Mark Edwards and George Tavard

AN ECUMENICAL STUDY GUIDE

FORTRESS PRESS, PHILADELPHIA
PAULIST PRESS, NEW YORK/RAMSEY

Published by Fortress Press, Philadelphia, Pennsylvania
and Paulist Press, New York/Ramsey

Library of Congress Cataloging in Publication Data
Edwards, Mark U.
     Luther, a reformer for the churches.
     1. Luther, Martin, 1483-1546.   I. Tavard, George H.
(George Henry), 1922–   .   II. Title.
BR325.E33 1983   284.1′092′4   83-14132
ISBN 0-8006-1718-5 (Fortress)
ISBN 0-8091-2575-7 (Paulist)

K361E83   Printed in the United States of America   1–1718

Contents

Forewords

I

On the occasion of the five-hundredth birthday of Martin Luther, Lutherans hope that together with the Roman Catholics the great importance of Martin Luther for all of us could be lifted up. Lutherans cannot, to be sure, escape the fact that they have at times made Luther into a hero instead of emphasizing that to which he devoted his life, the centrality of the gospel. It is salutary for Lutherans to see Luther as he really was, warts and all. On the other hand, Luther has not always been correctly appreciated by Catholics, and his theology has not always been correctly presented. Yet we note that in the last few decades Catholic scholars have come more adequately to understand the Reformation and consequently Luther and his theology.

For Lutherans this anniversary will be a time to study their origins and the central Christian truths which guide their lives. Roman Catholics also may find this anniversary year an occasion to reflect on the place of Martin Luther. Often he is remembered only for the forcefulness of his personality and his criticisms of the Roman Catholic church. Nevertheless, through common study with Lutherans, Roman Catholics today may be able to discover another side to Luther and may be able to overcome the hesitations they have naturally experienced in the past concerning Luther's life and work.

Luther was both a prolific genius and one who retained at the same time a considerable part of the Catholic faith. His work centered on one reality: the faith which justifies sinners and gives to our daily lives the true meaning and destiny intended by God. In the words of Jan Cardinal Willebrands to the Fifth Assembly of the Lutheran World Federation, Evian, France, July 15, 1970, we can learn from Luther ". . . that God must always remain the Lord, and that our most important human answer must always remain absolute confidence in God and our adoration of Him."

We are confident that common study and prayer in this anniversary year and beyond will be a great blessing for both of our Christian communities, and we recommend such joint study and prayer to the people of our churches.

The Reverend Dr. James R. Crumley, Jr.
Bishop of the Lutheran Church in America

The Reverend Dr. David W. Preus
Bishop of the American Lutheran Church

II

Only now, five hundred years after his birth, does it seem that Lutherans and Catholics might be able to come together in a shared effort to reach a common understanding of Martin Luther. To neither Lutherans nor Catholics has he ever been a minor or indifferent figure in the history of the church. But until the present era Catholics and Lutherans have had such very different pictures of the man, his life and his teachings that one could scarcely imagine them collaborating and publishing their views in a single volume.

The present work, the fruit of collaboration between a Lutheran and a Catholic author, is one sign of the steady growth of contact and exchange between the scholars of the two traditions over the past forty years. Its publication in the anniversary year is a source of encouragement.

To be sure, there is not yet a single view of Luther and a single interpretation of his major teachings that all Lutherans and Catholics share. No doubt Catholic readers will sense the hand of a Lutheran author giving shape to some of the chapters which follow, while Lutheran readers may be more alert to what they hear as a Catholic accent in other chapters. This is to be expected. For we all approach Luther through the filters of the intervening centuries which have colored our perception of him. It is well that at this stage the authors have not attempted to give us a completely smooth portrait of the man and his teachings in which no difference in Lutheran and Catholic perspective remains apparent.

They have provided an account which may prove more helpful, even if at times both Lutheran and Catholic readers will find themselves questioning what they have written. For by the same token the reader is likely to be surprised to learn things not previously known.

The effort that Lutherans and Catholics are making together to grasp anew the significance of Martin Luther and the reasons why his teachings have had such an immense impact is an effort to understand the history which has made us who we are. The better our grasp of this history, the better we shall understand who we are today and what our future as Christians may be.

The authors have shown a good deal of courage in facing even some of the most difficult and painful aspects of the past. But in the courage to face our past there is contained the hope and promise that we shall have the same courage to face our future together.

> Most Reverend John F. Whealon
> Archbishop of Hartford
> Chairman, Committee on Ecumenical
>   and Interreligious Affairs—
>   National Conference of Catholic
>   Bishops

1

Luther's World

It was already dark on April 18, 1521, when Brother Martin, freshly tonsured and wearing the brown habit of his Augustinian Order of Hermits, was led into a crowded and overheated room where the Imperial Diet of the Holy Roman Empire of the German Nation was in session. It was his second appearance in as many days before the emperor, princes, and officials of the empire. Two days earlier he had entered the city of Worms accompanied by an imperial herald and an escort of knights. According to the report of the papal representative in Worms, the legate Hieronymus Aleander, the populace had turned out to gawk at and cheer the heretic and to curse the pope, who had excommunicated Luther the year before. His journey from Wittenberg, where he was professor of Bible studies, to the imperial city of Worms had taken on the trappings of a triumphal procession. He had been feted by city councils, lauded by humanist orators, and now was applauded by the common people. To the legate's relief, however, Brother Martin did not fare so well in his first appearance before the Diet. Upon sight of the monk the emperor had reportedly exclaimed, "He'll make no heretic of me!" and the emperor's spokesman had insisted that Brother Martin answer to only two questions: First, were the more than twenty books piled there on a table his? Second, was he prepared to recant what he had written in them? Visibly nervous, Brother Martin had acknowledged in a low, hesitant voice that the books were his but asked for more time to consider his answer to the second question. He had been given twenty-four hours.

The twenty-four hours were now up, and Brother Martin was asked for his reply. His answer, given in both German and Latin and without the hesitation or faintness of the previous day, did not satisfy the imperial spokesman, and he was asked once again for a straightforward answer. Brother Martin replied:

Since then your serene majesty and your lordships seek a simple answer, I will give it. . . . Unless I am convinced by the testimony of the Scriptures or by clear reason (for I do not trust either in the pope or in councils alone, since it is well known that they have often erred and contradicted themselves), I am bound by the Scriptures I have quoted, and my conscience is captive to the Word of God. I cannot and I will not retract anything, since it is neither safe nor right to go against conscience. May God help me, amen.

After a few more exchanges with the imperial spokesman, he was led from the room. Some Spaniards in the emperor's entourage jeered and yelled "To the fire with him!" For his part Brother Martin raised his hands in the sign of victory and shouted "I am through; I am through." But in fact, Brother Martin Luther was not through. His reformation of the Roman Catholic church, what would come to be called the Protestant Reformation, was only just beginning.

This dramatic appearance before the Diet of Worms contains all the major elements of the first act of the Reformation. At the heart of the schism lay, of course, the understanding of Scripture and the Word of God explained in that pile of books at the Diet of Worms. Today Lutherans and Catholics are agreed on many points in those books that once divided them. Times have changed. And this means that to understand the splintering of Western Christendom that occurred in the sixteenth century, we must know something about the times in which Martin Luther lived and worked.

LATE MEDIEVAL PIETY AND BELIEFS

The late fifteenth and early sixteenth centuries saw a great upsurge in popular piety of a very churchly sort. People and organizations endowed Masses in ever-increasing numbers. They made numerous bequests to the church. They founded brotherhoods where they might pool their spiritual resources. They went on pilgrimages, visited relic collections, and venerated the saints. Often whole communities would embark on a pilgrimage or a religious project such as the building of a new church. Wealthy individuals spent great sums in the interest of their souls. Cardinal Albrecht of Mainz, for example, managed to accumulate 39,245,120 years credit against time he might have to spend in purgatory. While few others could acquire such spiritual wealth, they could at least leave a small bequest for Masses to be said after their deaths, and many took advantage of this opportunity.

Individual devotion also flourished. From 1450 to 1500 the bulk of the gigantic production of the newly invented printing press was devotional literature of a simple, traditional sort. During this period Germany also produced more printed translations of the Bible than did any other country. And partial editions of the Bible were even more numerous. By 1522 at least sixty-two complete or partial editions of the Psalms and one hundred thirty-one editions of the Gospel and Epistle readings for Sundays were printed. Given this massive production, lay people must have been buying and reading these works in great numbers.

There was another side to this religiosity. The late fifteenth century also saw the flaring of interest in occult forces. Fear of witchcraft was in the air, and the church itself took steps to deal with those thought to be trafficking with the devil. Hard-headed people of good education saw the devil's hand everywhere—in sickness, in storms, in monstrous births, and even in the petty accidents of everyday life. The devil was no abstraction, no comical red figure with a long tail, but rather the adversary, capable of possessing and using men and women to his own ends.

Many even feared, and half-hoped, that the world was reaching its end. The Turks, who threatened Christianity from the West, were popularly seen as harbingers of the end time. Men tried to calculate when the world would end, and interest in portents and prophecies was extraordinarily great.

Historians disagree whether all this interest in religion was wholesome or neurotic and whether it was mechanistic and external or individualistic and subjective. But they all recognize that even before the Reformation the sixteenth century was a highly religious age.

THE INSTITUTIONAL CHURCH

Although it did what it could, the institutional church was ill-equipped to respond to this lay religiosity. Parish priests normally did little more than read the Mass. This was really all they were qualified to do. Although between one-third and one-half of the priests in southern Germany had some university education, few had studied theology.

In any case, that still left one-half to two-thirds of the priests without university education. The conditions in northern Germany were even worse. When these priests did preach, the quality of their sermons was often shockingly low. And so when city guilds wished to provide preaching for their town, they bypassed the local clergy and brought in high-salaried, university-trained specialists.

The morality of the lower clergy was also often disappointingly low. Many priests kept "housekeepers," who in all but name and legal status were clerical wives. The practice was so common in the bishopric of Constance, for example, that the bishop took to taxing these arrangements. This is not a simple story of uncontrolled lust. In rural areas the family was the smallest viable economic unit; thus, to survive, the village priest frequently needed a helpmate and children.

The morality of the upper clergy also left much to be desired. The ecclesiastical princes imitated their secular brothers. They maintained enormous households, lived lavishly, and kept mistresses. Often singled out by their noble families for a clerical career at a very tender age, these young men were not asked whether they felt called to a life of chastity or whether they possessed an aptitude for spiritual matters. Under such circumstances, their shortcomings were perhaps predictable.

What was true for the bishops was also true for the popes. Since the popes were responsible for the preservation of the Papal States and were significant actors in the larger political drama of Europe, it is hardly surprising that the popes and leading papal officials of the pre-Reformation period owed their positions more to political and administrative acumen than to spiritual gifts. They lived like princes, thought like princes, and even fought like princes. The abuses of Rome were not unique. Other princes and their courts had many of the same problems. But of course more was expected of the papacy, and therefore it confronted the Reformation challenge with the handicap of a badly tarnished reputation.

The papacy was handicapped in other ways. The preceding century had opened with Western Christendom divided by the Great Schism. Not surprisingly, the spectacle of two and then three men each claiming to be the sole vicar of Christ and successor to St. Peter neither helped the reputation of the papacy nor bolstered its claims to the "fullness of power" over the church. The schism also saw the splintering of the papacy's administrative authority, with many of its rights and privileges being taken over by secular governments.

The schism was brought to a close by the Council of Constance (1414-1418). Since it was widely believed that the final authority within the church rested with the pope, it was necessary for the Council to declare that in emergency situations councils possessed authority superior even to the pope. On the basis of this claim, it deposed two papal claimants, accepted the resignation of a third, and elected a new pope. It also condemned and had burned the Czech heretics John Huss and Jerome of Prague. Finally, to provide some supervision for the papacy and to monitor reforms in the church, it further decreed that councils were to meet at regular intervals in the future.

This requirement for regular councils challenged papal claims to the "fullness of power" within the church and led ultimately to a serious clash between the papacy and the Council of Basel (1431–1449). By the early sixteenth century the papacy was firmly opposed to councils and had condemned all appeals from itself to a council. But many in Europe remained convinced that at least in some cases a council had authority equal or even superior to the pope.

Luther and the Reformation benefited from the difference of opinion on councils. From early in the history of the Reformation movement, many Germans felt that the only solution to the dispute was a council. Luther himself appealed to a council. But mindful of the struggle between popes and councils in the last one hundred years, successive popes resisted the call for a council to end the new schism engendered by the Reformation. When the papacy finally relented and convened the Council of Trent in 1545, too many years had passed to undo the divisions.

THE HOLY ROMAN EMPIRE OF
THE GERMAN NATION

In the sixteenth century the Holy Roman Empire of the German Nation comprised between two and three hundred independent and semi-independent states. Some of these states were large territories ruled by princes. Others were tiny and ruled by counts and imperial knights. There were some eighty-five imperial city-states ruled by city councils. And many of the territories, both large and small, were ecclesiastical states with bishops or abbots as their rulers. The emperor had only limited, carefully circumscribed authority over the constituent states of the empire. This fragmentation of sovereignty greatly favored the spread of the Reformation. It could and did proceed piecemeal, winning one state at a time. In nations such as France and England where one ruler had enormous authority over the affairs of the whole nation, the history of the Reformation was quite different.

The emperor of the Holy Roman Empire was elected. Since 1356 seven princes had been designated as "electors." They selected the emperor. Four of these electors were secular princes, the rulers of the Palatinate, Saxony, Brandenburg, and Bohemia, and three were ecclesiastical princes, the archbishops of Mainz, Trier, and Cologne.

In 1519, two years before the Diet of Worms, these seven electors had chosen a new emperor. The electioneering had been fierce. The two major candidates, Francis I, king of France, and Charles I, king of Spain, had spent enormous sums in the attempt to buy votes, and they had also promised numerous concessions to the princes in exchange for their support. Charles was elected, but the real winners were the princes who had lined their pockets and who had won valuable legal rights and privileges from their sovereign emperor.

This electioneering played a crucial role in the early Reformation. The pope was the head of Western Christendom. But he was also an Italian prince with territory, the Papal States, that crossed the Italian peninsula like a garter on a boot. Charles already ruled the land south of the Papal States. If he were emperor, he would also have claim to lands north of the Papal States. He would be the most powerful prince since Charlemagne, and a dangerous neighbor even for the pope. There was a long history of friction between emperors and popes, and, as a general rule, popes liked the emperors better weak than strong. So in the maneuvering to elect a new emperor the papacy had tried desperately to defeat Charles. Its candidates were Henry VIII, king of England, Francis I, king of France, and Frederick the Wise, elector of Saxony. But Frederick the Wise was also Martin Luther's prince! And thus during the crucial years of 1518 and 1519, Elector Frederick was able to prevail upon the papacy to handle Luther with more restraint and circumspection than would otherwise have been the case. Furthermore, as partial price for his election, Charles had promised that no German subject would be placed under the imperial ban without a hearing. To honor this promise Emperor Charles had to grant Luther a hearing at the Diet of Worms.

Within the empire territorial princes and city councils strove to extend their internal authority even as they resisted attempts by the emperor to subject them to his authority. These centralizing tendencies extended to the church. Although in theory the church was supposed to be independent of civilian control, in practice the state had by 1500 acquired considerable control over religion and church institutions within its borders. The Reformation was to benefit from, and also to further, this development. Even staunchly Catholic princes felt it proper to impose their wills on the church. This needs some explanation.

Most people were convinced in the sixteenth century that the well-being of a state depended upon the community maintaining a proper relationship with God. Rulers interfered with church matters at least in part because they believed quite sincerely that abuses or divisions within the church would invite God's wrath over the community. For the well-being of their subjects responsible rulers had to correct abuses and end divisions. It was this conviction that underlaid attempts at reform both before and after the outbreak of the Reformation.

CHARLES V AND THE HABSBURG EMPIRE

The young emperor at the Diet of Worms, Charles V of the house of Habsburg, was the last medieval emperor to seek with some hope of success the political and religious unity of Western Europe. He united in his person rule over Burgundy and the Netherlands, Spain, southern Italy, Sardinia, Sicily, the Balearic Islands, Austria, Spain's American possessions, and the Holy Roman Empire. No ruler since Charlemagne had possessed such territory.

But with the territory came enemies that were to bedevil Charles throughout his reign. In the East there were the Turks, who threatened by land and by sea. Charles's other great adversary was the "Most Christian King of France," Francis I, who did not scruple to make alliance with the Turks against his Habsburg rival. Repeatedly in the 1520s and 1530s Turkish and French attacks forced Charles to make concessions to the growing Protestant movement to secure their aid against his enemies. Moreover, to attend to his far-flung empire,

Charles was often away from Germany, giving the Protestants further opportunity to expand and consolidate their position within the Holy Roman Empire.

ANTI-ROMAN AND
ANTICLERICAL SENTIMENT

The cheers that greeted Luther when he rode into Worms were as much an expression of anticlerical sentiment as they were a sign of support for Luther's understanding of Christian theology. At all levels within German society and even among the clergy itself, there was much resentment toward Rome and the ecclesiastical hierarchy and a widespread conviction that the clergy needed to be put in its place. Repeated clashes between emperor and pope during the Middle Ages had left a tradition of hostility toward the papacy and Roman interference in German affairs. Abuses within the church and immorality among all ranks of the clergy added to the hostility and resentment. And many quarrels arose over the church's fiscal and legal arrangements.

Through the use of fines bishops often exercised control over the clergy and laity in their care. Clergy paid for such things as exemptions from regular duties, the right to collect alms, installation in office, and the keeping of "housekeepers." Laity paid fines to the bishop for absolution of "reserved sins" such as legitimation of adulterous offspring and absolution for homicide, public usury, blasphemy, and perjury. Lesser clergy, in turn, collected the tithe and charged the laity small fees for such services as performing the sacraments, for burials, and for saying Masses for the dead.

The institutional church was an independent corporation within the states of Western Christendom. It had its own law, its own courts, its own system of taxation. Normally it was exempt from the laws and taxes of the lay community of which it was a part. This exemption often led to bitter feelings, especially in the cities of the Holy Roman Empire where each citizen was expected to do his or her part for the common good. The bitterness was heightened when the clergy engaged in occupations that competed with lay businesses, such as the brewing of beer or the mending of shoes. In such cases their exemptions and immunities gave them, lay people felt, an unfair advantage.

These anticlerical sentiments had existed long before the Reformation and had led to frequent protests by the laity. The imperial diets had repeatedly passed lists of grievances against the clergy, yet the problem persisted. The Diet of Worms, which condemned Martin Luther, also issued a new set of grievances. Even many of those who disagreed with Luther felt that the church needed serious reform.

HUMANISM AND THE NEW LEARNING

On his way to Worms Luther had been greeted and praised by several prominent German humanists. These intellectuals saw in Luther another champion of a simple "lay" Christianity that stressed internal spiritual observances over external ones and that was based on a return to the sources of Christianity, that is, the Bible and the early church fathers. At the very least Luther was seen as another ally in the humanist struggle against "obscure men," mendicant friars, and Scholastic theologians who opposed the "new learning." These German Christian humanists had been among Luther's earliest and most important supporters. They had circulated the Ninety-five Theses in German translation far and wide over Germany. They had written treatises in support of Luther and had advocated his cause before city councils and in the chambers of princes. By 1521 many of the older humanists had begun to draw back from the radical course Luther was steering, but many of the younger humanists remained his staunchest allies and became in time leaders of the Reformation movement.

Although no humanist himself, Luther had benefited greatly from the humanist drive "back to the sources." He employed the latest scholarly aids, such as Reuchlin's Hebrew Grammar, Erasmus's edition of the Greek New Testament, and the recently published editions of the church fathers, especially St. Augustine. Luther helped lead a reform of the curriculum at the University of Wittenberg that stressed study of the classical languages, rhetoric, history, the early church fathers, and especially the Bible.

THE PRINTING PRESS

At the Diet of Worms Luther was asked to acknowledge as his own an enormous pile of books. He had written all these in a few short years, and by printing and reprinting they had spread all over the

Holy Roman Empire and beyond. The printing press played a crucial role in the genesis and spread of the Reformation.

Before the invention of printing with moveable metal type around 1450, books had to be copied by hand, and therefore they were very expensive and scarce. But printing and the development of cheap paper suddenly made it possible to reproduce a work thousands of times over and to sell this work at an affordable price. With the growth of a literate lay population about this same time, there was a ready market for the new invention. By 1500 there were printing presses in more than two hundred towns, and an estimated six million books had been printed. On the eve of the Diet of Worms there were printing establishments in sixty two German and Swiss cities, and these establishments were experiencing an incredible boom. Between 1518 and 1524, the revolutionary years of the Reformation, the printing industry in Germany increased its production sevenfold. Luther himself contributed mightily, authoring between 1517 and 1520 about thirty titles, which were printed in more than 300,000 copies. In an age before copyright laws, popular books spread by reprinting. And the demand for Luther's writings became so great and the competition between printers so fierce that some printers even printed works from copy stolen from Luther's "authorized" printers or even from Luther's own desk!

Perhaps four percent of Germany's population could read by 1500. But the production of the printing industry could reach a much wider audience than this. Many of the works were intended to be read aloud or were "targeted" at the "opinion leaders" of the sixteenth century: the preachers, lawyers, teachers, and rulers. There was also a lively trade in woodcuts, which presented in partisan pictures the great issues of the day.

Luther himself credited divine providence with the invention of printing at the very time that it was needed for the reform of the church. Certainly the Protestant demand that the church be measured by "Scripture" was greatly facilitated by the existence of a uniform printed edition of Scripture to which one could appeal. One of the first things Luther did after the Diet of Worms was to translate the New Testament into German. His German translation of the Bible became the "best-seller" of the sixteenth century.

FOR STUDY AND DISCUSSION

1. What two questions was Brother Martin asked at the Diet of Worms (1521), and how did he reply? Why did his reply to the second question not satisfy the imperial spokesman?

2. Describe some of the religious practices that characterized the "highly religious" period of the late fifteenth and early sixteenth centuries.

3. What were some of the features of the institutional church in the late fifteenth and early sixteenth centuries? Explain why the church was poorly equipped to respond to the people's popular religiosity.

4. Given the political situation in the Holy Roman Empire of the German Nation, how was it possible for Protestants to establish themselves and spread their cause within the empire?

5. What were some ways in which an anticlerical sentiment was expressed at this time, and how extensive was this sentiment?

6. Briefly explain the term "humanism" and state how Luther's efforts benefited from this intellectual movement.

7. What significance did the development of the art of printing have for the Reformation?

For Further Reading

Dickens, A. G. *The German Nation and Martin Luther*. London: Edwards Arnold, 1974.

Lau, Franz, and Ernst Bizer. *A History of the Reformation in Germany to 1555*. London: Adam & Charles Black, 1969.

Ozment, Steven. *The Age of Reform, 1250–1550: An Intellectual and Religious History of Late Medieval and Reformation Europe*. New Haven: Yale University Press, 1980.

Spitz, Lewis W. *The Renaissance and Reformation Movements*. 2 vols. St. Louis: Concordia Publishing House, 1980.

2

Luther's Life

By 1520 the Reformation movement was entering its third year, and
the charges facing Luther had grown serious enough to warrant burn-
ing if he fell into the wrong hands. One such accusation was that
Luther was a Bohemian and a follower of the Bohemian heretic John
Huss, who had died at the stake at the Council of Constance in 1415.
To answer this Luther wrote a letter to his friend and ardent supporter
George Spalatin, court chaplain and advisor to Luther's prince, Elector
Frederick the Wise. "I was born, by the way, at Eisleben, and bap-
tized there in St. Peter's Church," he told Spalatin (and all others with
whom Spalatin or the elector might wish to share this letter). "I do
not remember this, but I believe my parents and the folks at home."

The subtle irony of this comment is typical of Luther. The older
man, looking back on his youth and the years leading to his break with
Rome, often told his tale with a slightly roguish twinkle in his eye. In
his later years, the 1530s and 40s when the Reformation had captured
a significant portion of the empire and Luther had become for many
an outsized man—the greatest heretic of all times for some, a prophet
sent by God for others—he lived constantly in the public view. His
every comment at meals was zealously noted by attending students
and guests. His lectures and sermons were all taken down in short-
hand. His correspondents saved every letter they received from him.
As a result, we know what Luther did for twenty out of every thirty
days during the later years. From a distance of nearly five hundred
years, this is extraordinary! Yet there is a danger. Luther knew that
he had an audience. He knew that his life experiences were important
to others. So, on the one hand, he was not above testing with wry
humor the credulity of his audience; on the other hand, he was also
capable of shaping the facts of his early life to make a point, especially
a point about the horrors of the papacy under which he once lived. To

further complicate the biographer's task, in the years after his death new stories about his early life made their appearance in pious biographies by Lutherans and in hostile accounts by Catholics. A biographer, then, looking back on the life that led to the confrontation at the Diet of Worms is confronted with a confused mass of fact and fabrication. To disentangle the two is an almost impossible task. If in the following account you miss one of your favorite stories about Luther, blame it on the biographer's timidity. The story may be true, but then again, maybe not.

YOUTH

We do know that Luther was born in Eisleben on November 10. There is some debate about the year (Luther himself was unsure!) but 1483 is generally accepted. His father, Hans, was a copper miner, in time a mine operator of sufficient reputation to become a town councillor in Mansfeld, where the Luthers moved shortly after Martin's birth. His mother was born Lindemann, a leading burgher family in Eisenach. His father was hard-driving, going places, and nursed ambitions for his oldest surviving son: Martin was to be a lawyer. His mother may have strongly seconded these ambitions, given her family background. The Lindemanns sent their children to university; of Luther's cousins two became pastors; two, lawyers; one, a physician; two, schoolmasters; one, a university docent; and three, public officials. Luther's parents, and especially his mother, were pious, God-fearing people who raised their son with strictness but also with obvious love and warmth. Although Hans Luther came originally of peasant stock, Luther grew up in a solidly middle-class family.

Intended for a professional career, Luther was well schooled: seven years at the Latin school at Mansfeld, a year in Magdeburg, and three in Eisenach surrounded by his Lindemann kin. In 1501 he enrolled at the University of Erfurt. There he received his bachelor's degree in 1502 and his master's degree in 1505, finishing second among seventeen candidates.

In later life he remembered with disapproval an experience in Magdeburg when he was fourteen. There he saw a former duke of Anhalt who had abandoned the world for a life of penance and self-denial as a monk. To the older Luther, this was a deluded attempt at works-righteousness. To the adolescent boy, however, this must have seemed exemplary piety. Certainly the sermons he would have heard growing up stressed above all else the reality and unpredictability of one's own death and the imperative need to lead a life of contrition— a life of sincere, heart-felt sorrow for one's sins—a life conformed to the discipline of the church and to a search for grace through prayer, participation in the sacraments, fasting, and physical self-denial. The duke was living the ideal. In general Luther was a thoughtful young man, given to pondering the meaning of life; his friends at the university nicknamed him "the philosopher."

THE MONASTERY

It was probably this brooding thoughtfulness, fed by the many sermons on the nearness of death and God's demand for a life of repentance and galvanized into decision by a personal brush with death, that led Luther in the summer of 1505 to abandon his study of law and enter a monastery. Although his father strongly disapproved and questioned the soundness of Luther's decision, this step into the monastery was consistent with the best and all-but-universal thinking of the day that saw the monastic life as most pleasing to God, the foremost means to advance in charity, to become a true and acceptable child of God.

Luther became a monk in the belief that this vocation would most nearly assure his salvation. But his daily experiences as a monk left him in doubt. Was he truly in a state of grace? Had he confessed all his sins adequately? Was he becoming more loving and lovable? Would he die in grace? These were questions that could plunge Luther into despair to the point where he both feared and questioned the righteousness of a God who expected more of him than he could give despite all his efforts to meet God's requirements. These were questions that sent Luther to Scripture and to theologians asking hard questions about righteousness, sin, free will, and God's grace. These questions ultimately led him to a new understanding of justification (see below and chapter 3).

This monastic life did not mean, except figuratively, a complete flight from the world. Recognizing Luther's talents, his order, the Reformed Congregation of the Eremitical Order of St. Augustine, set him to study. In 1507 he was made priest and said his first Mass. He also returned to the classroom, to study and to teach. In 1508 he lectured briefly on the Nichomachean Ethics of Aristotle at the fledgling University of Wittenberg. Back in Erfurt he continued to study for his doctorate in theology, interrupted only by a brief journey on foot to Rome on business for his order. In 1511 he returned to Wittenberg; in 1512 he was made doctor of theology and immediately joined the faculty of the university. In later years when he was challenged for his presumption in attacking the teachings of the Catholic church, he found support and comfort in his doctoral oath to oppose "strange doctrines" that were "offensive to pious ears" and in his public call to teach at the university; he had only done, he claimed, what he had sworn and been called to do.

INDULGENCES AND THE BREAK
WITH ROME

Luther's responsibility as professor was to lecture on the Bible. From 1513 to 1515 he lectured on the Psalms, from 1515 to 1516 on Romans, from 1516 to 1517 on Galatians, and from 1517 to 1518 on Hebrews. In 1519 he began a second series of lectures on the Psalms. During these same years he was given considerable responsibility within his order and, from 1514, had the responsibility to preach in the Wittenberg parish church.

Until 1518 Luther was known only in academic and clerical circles. His lectures show him to be from the beginning a talented and original interpreter of the Bible. In his theology he largely had left behind the nominalism of his teachers and instead advocated an Augustinian approach to salvation, insisting that salvation depends entirely on the unmerited gift of God's grace. He and his colleagues at the little University of Wittenberg (enrollment about two hundred at the time Luther joined the faculty!) had also made a reputation for themselves for their advocacy of curriculum reform. They wished to replace the traditional study of Aristotle and scholastic theology with a curriculum based on the ancient sources, especially the Bible and the writings of the early church fathers such as Augustine. But it was not university reform or academic theology that propelled Luther from his "little corner" at Wittenberg onto the stage of world history; rather, it was a pastoral matter, his objection to a nearby sale of indulgences to members of his and other congregations.

Indulgences were tied to the sacrament of penance. A sinful Christian was expected to feel true sorrow for his sins, confess them to a priest, receive absolution, and then undertake the works of penance or satisfaction imposed by the priest. The works of satisfaction imposed on the penitent were limited, temporal penalties for the sins that, without the priest's absolution, would have condemned the individual to eternal punishment in hell. These works of satisfaction could be such things as special prayers, fasts, self-imposed corporal punishment, or pilgrimages. If a penitent failed to complete the satisfaction owed, he would suffer in purgatory for his omissions. By the later Middle Ages a penitent could purchase an indulgence, the money going to some "good cause" such as the construction of a church. The indulgence would release him from the satisfaction he owed by drawing on the "excess" merits of Christ and the saints to pay his "debt" to God. This "treasury of merits" was in the control of the pope, who could dispense from it as he saw fit. In addition, by Luther's day the church taught that indulgences also could be purchased by the living for those already in purgatory, thereby accelerating their journey to heaven.

On March 31, 1517, Pope Leo X authorized the primate of Germany, Archbishop Albrecht of Mainz, to sell throughout much of northern Germany the St. Peter's indulgence. The proceeds were to be divided between the construction of St. Peter's in Rome and the retiring of Albrecht's debts, which he had contracted in acquiring the Archbishopric of Mainz while being both underage and the possessor of two other bishoprics. In the late summer of 1517 the indulgence seller John Tetzel was peddling his wares just across the border from Electoral Saxony, and some of Luther's own parishioners crossed over to make a purchase.

From what he heard of Tetzel's sermons and what he read of the *Instruction* under which Tetzel was operating, Luther became convinced that the purchasers of the indulgences were being seriously misled, perhaps even to their damnation. So on October 31, 1517, he sent a humble but firm letter of protest to Archbishop Albrecht, enclosing with the letter a list of ninety-five theses on the power and efficacy of indulgences to show how problematic this sale of indulgences was. He also sent a copy of the letter and theses to his own bishop, Jerome Schulze of Brandenburg. The theses themselves were for academic debate. There is some doubt that the debate was ever held. Some historians also question the evidence for the posting of the Ninety-five Theses on the Wittenberg Castle Church door, the university's bulletin board!

Historians do know that when Luther wrote his Ninety-five Theses, he had no intention of breaking with the church or attacking the legitimate authority of the papacy. His concern was theological and pastoral. From his reading of Scripture, especially St. Paul, and his study of the early church fathers such as Augustine, Luther was convinced that the repentance that Christ taught was an unending life of repentance that expressed itself inwardly in the hatred of one's sinful self and outwardly in mortifications of the flesh. A Christian who is truly sorry for his or her sins seeks and desires punishment. To urge people to seek to escape punishment through indulgences is to lead them away from true repentance and into a dangerous, perhaps damning sense of false security. Good works of love were far preferable to indulgences. Luther denied that the pope had authority to release those in purgatory (except through prayers of intercession) or to forgive penalties that he himself had not imposed. To claim otherwise was to engender a false trust and to encourage people to lose the salutary and necessary fear of God.

By early 1518 the Ninety-five Theses had been made public, translated into German, and were circulating throughout the empire. Response was quick. Archbishop Albrecht sent the theses to Rome with a note suggesting that Luther was spreading "new teachings." Opponents, including John Tetzel, took up their pens to attack Luther, and the issue they seized on for their attack was not indulgences per se but the pope's power to grant indulgences. Against Luther's own wishes and expectation, the indulgence controversy was gradually transformed into a controversy over papal authority.

Driven step by step by opponents, Luther clarified his thinking on papal authority. Popes were men like any other men, he argued in early 1518, and could err in faith and morals; their opinions must be tested against Scripture, church fathers, and councils. In late summer 1518 he was challenged in writing by Sylvester Prierias, the pope's theological advisor, with the assertion that the head of the universal church is the pope who cannot err in matters of faith, that all those who fail to recognize this authority are heretics, and that even sacred Scripture draws its strength from the authority of the pope. Luther was unimpressed by this argument but disturbed that now the papacy itself had apparently taken a stand against him. On August 7, 1518, Luther received a summons to Rome, there to answer for his teachings. Elector Frederick was able, however, to transfer Luther's examination from Rome to Augsburg, where the imperial diet was meeting. In October Luther met in Augsburg with the papal legate and Thomistic theologian, Cajetan. In their meeting Cajetan answered Luther's appeal to Scripture and cogent reason with the assertion that the power of the pope was superior to councils, Scripture, and everything else in the church. Cajetan also challenged Luther's assertion that if a penitent trusted in Christ's words of forgiveness uttered by the priest in the sacrament of penance he or she could be certain of his or her forgiveness. No one could be certain of forgiveness, Cajetan insisted. On his way home from Augsburg Luther learned that the pope had ordered his arrest and recantation even before his meeting with Cajetan in Augsburg. In the aftermath of Augsburg, Luther appealed, first, from a badly informed pope to a better informed pope, then from the pope to a council.

It was in the midst of this controversy that Luther's understanding of justification by faith alone crystallized into his mature position (see chapter 3). Historians have spent endless hours and spilled oceans of ink on the exact timing and content of Luther's "Reformation breakthrough." Suffice it to say here that his theology developed over time. As Luther himself said, "I did not learn my theology all at one time; rather I had to dig for it ever deeper and deeper where my trials took me." Aspects of his mature position can be found in the earliest of his lectures, others make their appearance only after the outbreak of the indulgences controversy. But at some point, by Luther's report, they all came together and Luther experienced incredible relief. "Here I felt that I was altogether born again and had entered paradise itself through open gates!" Buoyed up by his discovery, he returned to the fray with renewed assurance. He would cling to his understanding even if it meant death or burning or exile. "It would be so easy to say 'I recant,' " Luther wrote his colleague Karlstadt on the eve of the third session with Cajetan. "But I will not become a heretic by recanting the belief that has made me a Christian."

By late 1519 Luther was beginning to share with close friends his suspicion that the antichrist predicted by St. Paul (2 Thess. 2:8) might be ruling in Rome. Although increasingly pessimistic about his chances of reaching an agreement, he continued to negotiate with Catholic authorities. By mid-summer 1519, however, prompted by an attack from the Catholic professor and theologian John Eck, he had gone public with his criticism of papal claims to authority. To Eck's claim that the pope and the Roman church had always been superior to all other churches and that the pope was Christ's vicar on earth, Luther insisted that the history of the last fifteen hundred years, the Council of Nicea, and the Scripture itself all proved otherwise. Not only could popes err, their claim to rule by divine right was a fraud perpetrated by "flatterers" of the pope. In debate with Eck at Leipzig in early July 1519, Luther went one step further when he asserted that not only popes, but also councils could err. Specifically, the Council of Constance had erred when it had condemned several articles of the Bohemian Huss, which were "most Christian and evangelical." Scripture had become the sole touchstone by which all other authorities were judged.

The year 1520 saw Luther and the Roman church take their final leave of each other. For his part Luther published a series of treatises that spelled out his understanding of true Christianity and attacked all the perversions that he believed the papacy, the antichrist, had introduced into the church. The three greatest of these treatises were calls for renewal within Christianity and for resistance against papal tyranny: *To the Christian Nobility of the German Nation Concerning the Reform of the Christian Estate; On the Babylonian Captivity of the Church;* and *The Freedom of a Christian.*

On October 11, 1520, Luther received the papal bull *Exsurge, Domine,* threatening him with excommunication if within sixty days he had not recanted. On December 10 the students of the University of Wittenberg were invited to witness "a pious and religious spectacle, for perhaps now is the time when the antichrist must be revealed." A bonfire was kindled outside the gates of the town and Martin Luther committed the bull to the flames. On January 3, 1521, he was formally excommunicated by the pope.

The next step for his Catholic opponents was to have Luther placed under the imperial ban, that is, declared an outlaw. But according to the agreements that Emperor Charles had reached with the princes as a partial price of his election, no subject could be placed under the ban without a formal hearing. While the behind-the-scenes maneuvering was fierce, Luther's prince, Elector Frederick, was able to secure a hearing for Luther at the imperial diet meeting in Worms.

Luther's appearance before the Diet of Worms (see chapter 1) marks the end of the first phase of the Reformation movement. Against his will Luther had been expelled from the Roman Catholic church. But the task of reforming the church had just begun.

DEFINING A MOVEMENT

On his journey home from the Diet of Worms, Luther was "kidnapped" by some of Elector Frederick's men and spirited away to the Wartburg, one of the elector's castles, to keep him safe from the hands of Catholic authorities. After the hectic pace of the last several years, his stay at the Wartburg gave him the time to think and also to brood, to gain weight, and to become sick. In later years Luther suffered from similar bouts of depression (battles with the devil, he called them), and he was often gnawed by the question, "Are you alone wise?" The emaciated monk gave way over the years to the fat doctor. And his health, delicate even as a monk, gradually declined. In later years he suffered from constipation, diarrhea, hemorrhoids, dizziness and ringing in his ears, an ulcer on his leg, kidney stones, and heart problems.

But depression, over-eating, and ill health hardly slowed his enormous productivity. Excluding Bible translations, Luther produced some three hundred and sixty published works from 1516 to 1530. From 1531 to his death in 1546 he added another 184 publications to this incredible total. At the same time he lectured regularly at the university, preached for long stretches in the parish church, wrote hundreds of letters, advised his princes in numerous written memoranda, and closely followed the events of his day. The critical edition of his works runs to well over one hundred large folio volumes! The following overview cannot even touch on all the highlights of his later years.

While at the Wartburg Luther continued the process of spelling out and justifying the reforms that flowed, inexorably he felt, from his understanding of justification by faith alone. He wrote a commentary on the Magnificat, honoring Mary as the Mother of God while insisting on the exclusive role of grace in her elevation. He wrote a treatise on confession in which he rejected mandatory confession even as he recommended voluntary confession as an aid to troubled consciences. In another treatise he rejected monastic vows and enforced clerical celibacy as species of works-righteousness that deluded people into looking to themselves rather than to Christ for salvation. All vocations were equal in God's sight if done in faith and with love for one's neighbor. Celibacy was a gift God gave to a few; it was praiseworthy but it contributed nothing to salvation. He also continued work on his Psalms commentary, wrote a wonderful collection of sermons for the Advent season, and lashed out in several treatises against Catholic opponents. Most significant of all, he translated the New Testament into German for all Germans to read in their mother tongue.

In the spring of 1522 Luther returned to Wittenberg to bring under control a reform movement that had become unruly (see chapter 5). Once back, he was home to stay. Except for several short trips and a more extended stay at the Castle Coburg in 1530 during the Diet of Augsburg, he was to live the rest of his life in Wittenberg.

Once back, Luther steered the reform movement in a more moderate direction. He was basically a conservative, preserving the status quo except where he felt that the gospel demanded otherwise and moving slowly even then. He rejected the idea of the Mass as a sacrifice, the doctrine of the transubstantiation of the bread and wine into the body and blood of Christ, the practice of private Masses where there were no communicants, and the withholding of the communion cup from the laity. Yet he instituted each of these reforms only after considerable instruction from the pulpit and only after the laity had been given time to adjust to the changes. In his German Mass he retained as much of the traditional ceremony as he could.

Attempts by Catholic princes, such as Duke George of Saxony, to restrict access to Luther's German Bible and other harassments of Protestant laity by Catholic rulers led Luther in 1523 to issue an important treatise, *On Secular Authority: To What Extent it Should be Obeyed.* He argued that God had established two "kingdoms." Within the spiritual kingdom God rules through the Word, the gospel of Christ. Within the worldly kingdom, God rules through secular authorities, who bear the sword. God is Lord of both kingdoms and rules in both, but they must not be confused. Secular authorities with their sword should not meddle in the spiritual kingdom where the Word is the only coercive force; similarly, the ministers of the Word should not meddle in the secular kingdom where the sword coerces evil doers. Where there is a mixing, there you can find Satan at work. Under this schema Luther was able on the one hand to attack the papacy for meddling in secular matters and on the other hand to criticize the peasants a few years later for attempting to use the gospel to support their secular demands (see chapter 5).

In 1524 and 1525 he was forced to respond to the first major splits within the Protestant ranks and to the popular uprising known as the Peasants' Revolt (see chapter 5). At the peak of the uprising and expecting imminent death, Luther decided to offer Satan further defiance: he married. He had advocated marriage for other clerics for nearly five years, but for a variety of reasons he had hesitated to practice what he preached. In 1523 he had indirectly assisted twelve nuns to escape from a convent near Grimma. Three returned to their families. For eight of the remaining nine Luther found suitable husbands, but for the ninth, Katherina von Bora, he found no one she would accept besides Wittenberg's pastor, John Bugenhagen, and himself. And thus at age forty-two he married twenty-six-year-old Kate, not out of love or sexual desire, but to please his father who liked the idea of grandchildren, to spite the pope who forbade clerical marriage, and to witness to his convictions before his martyrdom! From this inauspicious beginning there did develop bonds of love and respect. The Protestant parsonage found its first model. The Luthers had six children, four of whom survived to adulthood. Kate Luther took over the management of the former Augustinian cloister where Luther lived. In later years it always teemed with student boarders, orphaned relatives, and frequent long- and short-term guests, and Kate kept it running despite her husband's imprudent generosity, which, on occasion, threatened to break the Luthers' meager budget. She ran the house, her domain, with firmness. Punning on her name, Luther occasionally called her teasingly "my chain" *(mea catena)* and "my lord." But he displayed his deep affection for his wife when he called his favorite Pauline epistle, the letter to the Galatians, "my Katherina von Bora." No feminist in the twentieth-century sense, he nevertheless had a very high regard for women, for marriage, and for sexual relations within marriage. The misogyny of the Middle Ages found little echo in Luther.

In 1525 Luther published *On the Bondage of the Will*, his reply to *On the Freedom of the Will* by the great humanist, Erasmus (see chapter 3). The next several years saw the development of the vituperative conflict with the Swiss and South German Protestants over the Lord's Supper (see chapter 5).

BUILDING A CHURCH

In the later years of the decade the Reformation movement began the transition from movement to institution. It is one thing to formulate a new vision of the Christian faith and quite another to give this vision form so that it may be passed on to one's children and one's children's children. Beginning in the late 1520s Luther and his supporters began the task of creating the Lutheran church.

First there was the need to define Lutheran beliefs. In 1529 Luther issued the *Small* and *Large Catechisms* to bring the fundamentals of Lutheran Christianity to a population that in distressing numbers was ignorant of even the basics of Christianity. In 1530 his colleague and co-worker Philipp Melanchthon penned an enduring summary of the Lutheran faith to be presented to the emperor, the *Augsburg Confession*. Meant to approach the Catholic position as closely as possible without surrendering any crucial issue, the *Confession* laid out concisely the areas of agreement and disagreement. No mention was made of the pope. Seven years later, when the possibility of reconciliation seemed remote and the need for diplomacy less urgent, a new section was added rejecting papal claims of authority within the church and the world and identifying the papacy with the antichrist.

As the institution developed, the politicians gradually took over. In 1531 the League of Schmalkalden was formed to defend the Protestant states against possible Catholic attack. In 1535 the papacy finally announced its intention to convene a general council of the church to settle the schism. It took in fact another ten years for the council actually to convene at Trent. This papally controlled council was rejected by the Protestant princes for both religious and political reasons, although their theologians, including Luther, argued that they should attend. In 1536 the Lutherans and Southern Germans reached a concord on the Lord's Supper that, not incidentally, also regularized the military alliance between the two. In 1539 war threatened between the Protestant and Catholic estates, and the League of Schmalkalden skirmished with the Catholic Duke Henry of Brunswick-Wolfenbüttel in 1542 and again in 1545.

Luther was much involved in these political maneuverings, but he also continued his theological and pastoral labors. In 1534 he and his colleagues completed their German translation of the Bible. Luther lectured regularly, helping the University of Wittenberg prepare the hundreds of new pastors needed to bring the Reformation down to the grass roots. In 1539 he produced his masterwork *On the Councils and the Church*, in which he spelled out his understanding of councils and church from the standpoint of Scripture and history.

Luther was profoundly disquieted by events in these later years, seeing everywhere the signs that the end of the world was at hand. To do his part in these final days, he issued ferocious "last testaments" against the papacy, the Turks, the "fanatics," and the Jews. Yet despite his pessimism and discouragement, Luther remained involved and productive to his death. He preached and lectured, wrote treatises and letters, and offered advice and counsel to princes and common people. Finally, while in Mansfeld settling a feud between the local counts, he died of heart failure on February 18, 1546. One of the last things he jotted down was his musing about the limits of our knowledge:

> No one can understand Vergil in his *Bucolics* unless he has been a herdsman for five years.
> No one can understand Vergil in his *Georgics* unless he has been a farmer for five years.

No one can fully understand Cicero in his letters unless he has spent twenty-five years in a great commonwealth.

Let no one think that he has sufficiently tasted Holy Scripture, unless he has governed the churches with the prophets, such as Elijah and Elisha, John the Baptist, Christ, and the apostles, for a hundred years.

Touch not this divine *Aeneid.*

Rather, fall on your knees and worship at its footsteps.

We are beggars, that's the truth.

(Table Talk, No. 5677)

FOR STUDY AND DISCUSSION

1. How reliable are the accounts of Luther's life?

2. Where was Luther born and on what date? Describe Luther's family—father, mother, other relatives.

3. What schools did Luther attend, and what was the original goal of his studies? What kind of student was Luther? What prompted him to enter monastic life? In what year was he ordained a priest? How much later did he earn his doctorate in theology?

4. What specific issue propelled Luther from his "little corner" at the University of Wittenberg onto the stage of world history, and what point was Luther trying to make regarding this issue?

5. Describe the immediate situation that moved Luther to draft his Ninety-five Theses. What was the main point of the Theses, and how did church leaders respond to the Theses?

6. What was the name of the papal legate who opposed Luther at the Diet of Augsburg (1518)? What issue was under debate at the diet? Contrast Luther's position on this issue with that of the papal legate.

7. How did Luther respond to the papal bull of 1520 that threatened him with excommunication? What is the date of his formal excommunication by the pope, and what did it mean for Luther to be placed under the "imperial ban"?

8. What happened to Luther on the journey home from his hearing at the Diet of Worms? Describe Luther and his productivity during the years at the Wartburg. When did Luther return to Wittenberg, and how long did he remain there?

9. Explain the comment that Luther "was basically a conservative." What was the point of his "two kingdoms" argument?

10. Describe Luther's marriage, family, and home. Recount some of the significant events in Luther's life from the late 1520s until his death on February 18, 1546.

For Further Reading

Bainton, Roland. *Here I Stand: A Life of Martin Luther*. Nashville: Abingdon Press, 1950.

Haile, H. G. *Luther: An Experiment in Biography*. New York: Doubleday & Co., 1980.

Hendrix, Scott. *Luther and the Papacy: Stages in a Reformation Conflict.* Philadelphia: Fortress Press, 1981.

Lohse, Bernhard. *Martin Luther: An Introduction to His Life and Work.* Philadelphia: Fortress Press, forthcoming.

Manns, Peter, and Helmuth Nils Loose. *Martin Luther: An Illustrated Biography.* New York: Crossroad, 1982.

Oberman, Heiko. *Luther: A Man Between God and the Devil.* New Haven: Yale University Press, forthcoming.

Schwiebert, E. G. *Luther and His Times: The Reformation from a New Perspective.* St. Louis: Concordia Publishing House, 1950.

Siggins, Ian. *Luther and His Mother.* Philadelphia: Fortress Press, 1981.

Todd, John. *Luther: A Life.* New York: Crossroad, 1982.

3

Luther's Central Insight

From the first moment they started preaching the "good news" of the resurrection of Christ, Christians have followed the gospel. The term itself (*evangelion* in Greek), which has always been in use, has helped Christians differentiate themselves from Jews, who follow the Old Testament, and from Moslems, who follow the Koran. Christians instead follow the gospel, which can designate the four books of the New Testament that outline the origin, ministry, death, and resurrection of Jesus. In a broader sense, however, it means all that can be known of Jesus if these four Gospels are put together. Still more broadly, "gospel" can be taken as identical with all the New Testament or as designating the sum total of the Christian faith. Can it also designate a doctrine?

Martin Luther generally equated the gospel with a doctrine, but really more than a mere doctrine; the gospel means justification by faith, and justification by faith is the heart of the Christian experience. Luther did not wish to select arbitrarily one doctrine and make it superior to others. His intent was to identify the center of Christianity, that aspect of the work of Christ and the Holy Spirit without which no doctrine, however well attested and universally or solemnly taught, makes any sense. He wanted to find the knot that ties all the aspects of Christianity together, the point of convergence or the focus of all the Scriptures and all the authentic traditions of the Christian church.

JUSTIFICATION BY FAITH

Justification by faith described for Luther the point where God's act of redemption (itself the purpose of the incarnation) coincides with its effect in the believer. God gives and one receives. Just as God gives life in creation and the creature's reception of this gift is its very life, so God through the dying and rising of Christ and in the power of the Holy Spirit gives new life, and its reception by the faithful is this very life. But what is the gift? What is this life?

Luther's spiritual experience had convinced him that nothing in the process of salvation comes from us. If it came from us, it would not be God's total gift. What derives from us bears the mark of original and personal sin and is therefore sinful. Only God gives new life. In God's plan this new life is that of Jesus, the Word incarnate. By its gift we are justified, made just, in God's eyes. For now God looks at us through Jesus Christ, seeing in us a righteousness, a holiness, that is not ours but that belongs to the incarnate Word, the Savior. Because this gift of justification exists for us only in Jesus Christ, it is called justification by faith. Faith means belief in what God reveals of himself in Jesus Christ. But this is not merely an intellectual exercise. It involves a commitment of one's own self, of all that one is and one has, to the Savior and his redeeming action.

Luther had personally experienced the danger of relying on oneself, on one's efforts and intents, on one's good resolutions and achievements. Relying on himself and failing to carry through, he had been led to despair by an unsteady mixture of faith and of reliance on his own good works. Faith should lead to hope, but it can do so only if one does not count on oneself at all for salvation. In this way Luther was led to realize that the faith through which one is justified in God's eyes is *faith alone:* a faith that relies solely, exclusively, on the gift from God made to us in the person, the life, the death, and the resurrection of Jesus Christ. Thus faith alone implies *grace alone.* For it is all gift, an undeserved, unmerited raising to new life. And by the same token it also means *Christ alone.* For this new life exists nowhere but in Jesus Christ.

The faith that justifies is belief; it implies believing the truth of what God has done and revealed in Jesus Christ and which one is led to accept by the Holy Spirit. But it is also trust; I trust that this act of God in Jesus Christ is not an abstraction, a remote event vaguely remembered, but that it is real for me now in my life. As the *Large Catechism* (The Apostles' Creed, Second Article) expresses it, "What does it mean that Jesus Christ becomes Lord? It means that he has freed me from sins, from the devil, from death, and from all harm." As a result of this trust, faith is more personalized in its effects than when faith is conceived only as belief. All that God does is "for me." The believer experiences personal assurance of salvation. But this should not be misunderstood. It is not that I am saved by a revelation. It is in fact closely related to the medieval understanding of hope, for it is more like a hope which is already fulfilled in the present.

Justification by faith, or, as one can also express it, by grace through faith, becomes in Luther's writings a key to all Christian life and doctrine. It is a key to Christian living. For once it has been understood and practiced, it replaces the need for systems of commands and prohibitions telling one what to do and what to avoid. The tasks of this world are still pursued, and the laws of society respected, but in a new spirit.

It also is a key to all doctrine. For everything that is formulated in the traditional creeds is to be understood in the light of the central fact of justification by faith. It is thus a Christian truth, but it is not philosophical or even religious truth in the wider sense. It is, rather, the truth of the gospel, the truth that flows from the gospel. Theology, traditionally described, is "faith seeking understanding," yet such an understanding is not an achievement of scholars. It originates in the gospel, in the experience of justification by faith alone. All the doctrines of the creed, all the explanations of the sacraments, all the developments of dogma through the ages need to be understood in its light. Theology is no longer a scholastic synthesis. It is not a structure of the mind. It is the act by which one brings justification by faith to bear on all the problems that may arise in the course of human existence.

THEOLOGICAL METHOD

Luther was by training a professor of Scripture. His personal interests had made him conversant with the literature of Christian mysticism, and he had published two editions of the *Theologia Germanica*, an anonymous writing from the school of the Rhineland mystics. The theology he had studied was that of nominalism, a late medieval form of Scholasticism. The spiritual tradition of the Augustinian Order had also given him a deep grounding in the theology of St. Augustine with its emphasis on grace and its running battle with all forms of Pelagianism (or the reliance on oneself for salvation). His writings show both the continuing influence of these sources on his thought and various forms of reactions against them.

In reading the biblical texts, Luther no longer followed the medieval practice of looking for spiritual senses that could be added to the literal meaning by the reader's insight or ingenuity. Rather, the literal meaning itself, as it emphasizes the work of Christ, is spiritual. And Luther spent most of his life translating the Bible, preaching and commenting upon it. In doing theology, he was no longer interested in the questions and distinctions that were at the heart of the Scholastic method of argumentation. He was profoundly dissatisfied with the answers and solutions proposed by the nominalist theologians. Theology must discover a new method, one which would flow from the central principle of justification by faith. But Luther by temperament was neither speculative nor systematic; he never fully explained the method, though he hinted at it. He certainly practiced it. In systematics Luther tended to rely on others, and the first truly systematic work based on justification by faith was not done by him, but by his friend and follower, Philipp Melanchthon.

The Reformer also implied a new theological method when he contrasted two types of theologians. There is the "theologian of glory" who seeks to elaborate on the gospel with his own science and scholarship and thus, with the help of philosophy and the logic of natural reason, introduces distinctions, makes deductions, and reaches conclusions. But since the subject matter of this exercise is the gospel, the gospel is lost in the process. By contrast, the "theologian of the cross" is content with confronting all reality, empirical or scientific, individual or social, with the paradox that on the cross the Word made flesh died "for us and for our salvation." This theology tries to place all things under the cross of Jesus. In its light one does not discover the inventions of one's mind but the reality of things as they are in the world as it is. Without Jesus Christ and the cross through which he went to the resurrection, this reality is distorted by sin. Under the cross of Christ, however, human existence in this sinful world is redeemed; one is justified by faith; through it one passes from death to life, from the death of this world to the life of the Risen One.

LAW AND GOSPEL

Luther expressed his central insight in other ways as well. Of special importance is the distinction which he made between the law and the gospel. As Luther advanced in age, he found himself involved in polemics not only with those who out of conscience or convenience preferred the security of the late medieval church structure and the guidance of the bishops, especially of the bishop of Rome. He also fought with the Swiss reformer Ulrich Zwingli and his followers, who differed from Luther on the Eucharist; with some of his own early partisans, who considered Luther too conservative in matters of liturgy and social order; and, later, with those in Lutheran lands who were influenced by the theology of Calvin. In the course of his early polemics, Luther emphasized St. Paul's message that with the coming of the gospel the law has been abolished. A particularly bitter polemic had to do with the consequences of this principle. To what extent is the Christian free? Luther liked to say that there is no freedom in the intellect: human reason, left to itself, is a harlot. Likewise, human will, left to itself, is unfree. But a new world opens up to both the mind and the will by reason of the gospel. Once we are justified by faith, to what extent are we really free?

It was the Peasants' Revolt that raised the question of Luther's understanding of Christian freedom. That justification by faith brings with it as its sequel freedom is clear, for the law has been abolished. Luther on this point repeated Paul's message. He even radicalized it, affirming that the law that has been abolished includes even the Ten Commandments. For those who are in Christ, all is gospel; there is no law. In Luther's mind, however, this freedom cannot be used selfishly because it is freedom in Christ. The faithful, in that which pertains to them rather than to Christ, remain sinners. A Christian is both and at the same time "justified and sinful." As just, one is freed by grace; as sinful, one is a slave to sin. The result of the freedom brought about by the gospel is not licentiousness or lawlessness; it is a new obedience, a new kind of obedience. This obedience does not result from fear of the law and its punishments but from the love which follows in the wake of faith.

Certainly the Peasants' Revolt cannot be fully explained by a mis-understanding of what Luther meant. Social conditions of oppression lay at the root of the revolt, but it found theological support in the rejection by some of Luther's early disciples of the second half of the slogan: justified and sinful. For Luther the law has not been replaced by human ambitions and the will to power. Antinomianism (or the theory that the law is in one's own hands) forgets that in such adages as "justified and sinful," "law and gospel," the two terms stand to-gether even at the point where the sinful become justified, where the gospel replaces the law.

THREE TRACTATES

Among all of Luther's works, three relatively short tractates composed in 1520 provide a succinct exposition of the theology inspired by the central insight of justification by faith. His *Treatise on the Freedom of a Christian* is generally acclaimed as a classic of the spiritual life. It is centered on the famous statement, "A Christian is a perfectly free lord of all, subject to none. A Christian is a perfectly dutiful servant of all, subject to all." Not polemical in tone and dedicated to Pope Leo X, who is even compared to "Daniel in Babylon" and to "a lamb in the midst of wolves," the treatise describes the spiritual situation of Christians who through the power of faith trust totally in God, not in self or in achievements; who honor and worship the Lord; and who are led to a royal marriage with the Bridegroom. Through baptism and faith we are made kings and priests. Kingship implies freedom and priesthood consists in prayer. Within this priesthood of all be-lievers there is a task of ministry and a stewardship that cannot belong to all and for whom some are chosen; this is a service, not a lordship. Luther also explains the right place of good works in Christian life, for these proceed from faith and have no saving power of their own. They are not done by fear and under duress but "freely and joyfully for the sake of others." Christians find a way between those who despise ceremonies and those who give them excessive importance, between those who reject all obedience and those who obey out of fear. They do not need an outward law because another law has been written in their hearts.

Other writings of the same year have a more polemical tone. *To the Christian Nobility of the German Nation* is fundamentally a call for a council that will reform the church and settle pending questions. Unlike the organization of general councils in the Middle Ages but similar to those of patristic times, Luther wants the secular princes, not the pope, to take on the responsibility for such a council. Three walls need to be destroyed, Luther explains: the wall of separation between the secular and the ecclesiastical, the wall that reserves to the Roman hierarchy the interpretation of Scripture, and the wall that separates the pope from everybody else by giving him an authority that cannot be questioned. Luther then lists a number of topics touching church reform that ought to be examined in a council. He ends with some twenty-seven concrete proposals that could be implemented by the princes while waiting for a council.

If *To the Christian Nobility* is the most controversial of these writings from the point of view of papal authority, the treatise on *The Babylonian Captivity of the Church* implies a more direct attack on certain aspects of medieval teaching. This pamphlet stems directly from the quarrel over indulgences (see the discussion of indulgences in chapter 2). Luther rightly saw that such a system was defensible only if the good works of the saints are meritorious in themselves. But this ran contrary to his understanding of faith and to the sovereignty of Christ as the only redeemer and mediator. Luther had seen the dire consequences of the system in popular piety, for simple people thought they could pay their way out of purgatory by having the merits of the saints applied to themselves. And since this lay behind the preaching of an indulgence for building the great church of St. Peter at the Vatican, he could not separate the bishop of Rome and his power from the indulgence and merit system.

In *The Babylonian Captivity of the Church* Luther examines the medieval doctrine of the seven sacraments and its ties to the prevailing understanding of merit and indulgences. He retains only baptism, the Eucharist, and penance as scriptural sacraments, for all three correspond to divine promises made in the gospels. But he criticizes the way in which these have been lately understood. Thus he believes the Lord's Supper has been distorted because the Mass has been identified as a good work and defined as a sacrifice for sins; there is no sufficient reason why transubstantiation, which he regards as a scholastic theory, should be imposed on the faithful as a matter of conscience. Yet, as is made clear in his controversy with Zwingli in 1529, Luther fully maintains the real presence of the body and blood of Christ in the Sacrament. As to baptism, its effects have been misunderstood, as can be seen in the practice of religious vows, considered by some to constitute a second baptism. But this lessens the importance of true baptism in the death and resurrection of Christ. Penance also has been distorted by being compartmentalized into contrition, confession, and satisfaction. It is strange, however, that Luther says nothing of what was in fact the most important aspect of penance, namely, absolution. One may also note that he goes back to the old medieval practice of confession to lay people when he proposes that anyone who has faith can be a confessor.

As to the other four sacraments, they are not, in Luther's mind, divinely instituted. Confirmation and extreme unction are superfluous. Marriage should be left to the state for its regulation. Ordination, useful for the designation of the ministers of the gospel, should not be understood to be a sacrament; it does not carry with it the promise of justification.

FREE WILL

Another writing, published a few years later, should be looked at here, since it completes Luther's doctrinal synthesis. This is his tractate on *The Bondage of the Will* (1525), which was prompted by a defense of *The Freedom of the Will* written by the famed Renaissance humanist, Erasmus. Here Luther draws the consequences of justification by faith alone for the powers of the human will left to itself. Just as the human reason is unable by itself to arrive at a saving knowledge of God, the human will is unable by itself to perform any good work that has value for salvation. The proper domain of both is the world with its secular purposes and achievements. In anything connected with salvation the human will is powerless and dominated by sin. Choice is not the kind of language that is appropriate to salvation. The justified do not start from freedom of choice, but rather from the bondage of their wills to evil. At least since St. Augustine this was implied in the doctrine of original sin. But it had been watered down in medieval Scholasticism, which, with its teaching on different kinds of merit, assigned some responsibility to the will in obtaining grace and salvation. As Luther perceived it, this endangered the sovereignty of God and the gift-character of grace. If justification is due, be it only in part, to the human will and its freedom, it is not entirely due to the Savior. This is of course connected with a doctrine of predestination; God not only foreknows but even predestines the elect to heavenly glory. Predestination had caused no problem when it was held by medieval theologians such as Thomas Aquinas. It had been a point of contention only when it was paired with a doctrine of eternal reprobation. But such a "double predestination" was not taught by Luther. What predestination implies from a religious point of view is simply that all is in the hands of God, especially the salvation of the elect. Predestination should inspire trust, not fear.

FUNCTIONS OF JUSTIFICATION

This brief survey of the first reform writings of Luther should enable us to assess the true scope of justification by faith as the expression of the Christian gospel. It is a doctrine, since it can like all doctrine be given a formulation, be intellectually understood, and be accepted in one's confession of faith. It can be paid lip-service, and it can be internalized. But it is more than a doctrine because it underlies all that can be said about the Christian faith and life. Its foundational function can be understood along several lines.

Justification by faith can be read as a methodological principle. In this case it has to do with the way theology is done, with the tone in which the gospel is proclaimed and the articles of the creed are taught, and even with the way in which the church functions as a community proclaiming the kingdom of God. A method is an organized way of operating by which one makes progress from point A to point B through a series of related steps that have a cumulative effect as each one builds on the one before. A principle concerning the method of the Christian life regulates the steps that one undergoes as one enters the Christian community and lives within it in keeping with the gospel preached by the community. But these steps in fact have a long history that one can study, for instance, in relation to baptism and Christian initiation. And the history shows that none of these steps is simply identifiable with the gospel. Thus understood as a principle regulating a method, justification by faith reminds us that faith is both within and beyond every formulation of it in words or in deeds. Since this is the case, then it also means that each and all of the elements which identify the Christian community as Christian should of themselves promote justification by faith. Moreover, they should always remain open to the judgment that they are not sufficiently transparent to the purpose of God. At the heart of the church, then, the principle of justification by faith should function as does grammar in relation to language. Grammar is not the whole language, but the regulating principle that controls both the use of words and their relationships in meaningful sentences.

Justification by faith can also function as an exegetical principle. That is, the Scriptures of the Old and the New Testaments can be read in its light. When this is done, it becomes clear that the principle replaces neither historical or textual studies nor the scholarly disciplines that help in understanding the meaning of texts in their original setting. But once the historical or literal sense has been ascertained, it still remains to be seen how this sense relates to the Christian message. This is where justification by faith enters. It helps one to gauge the dimensions of the text as law and as gospel; to explain its connection with the center of the gospel, Jesus Christ; to show how the text and its meaning have continuing relevance for Christian faith and life; to rely on Christ alone and not on oneself; to adopt the receptive attitude called for by the gift of God in Jesus Christ; to elicit the feelings of trust and thanksgiving with which the righteousness of Christ should be viewed by a sinful human; and to proceed in new obedience and love to the good works that will testify to the righteousness of Christ and its effective influence in one's life. In other words, justification by faith as an exegetical principle will make it possible for the gospel not to be understood as an abstraction, a universal philosophical axiom, or a requirement of all human existence, but rather as what God has done and still is doing in Jesus Christ for me and for all sinners like me.

It follows from both these uses that the principle of justification also develops into a critical principle, one that allows us to look at ourselves, as it were, from a distance so that we can assess ourselves and our situation. It enables the onlooker to be free from the weight of habit, custom, and prejudice that normally impedes frank and honest judgments. Insofar as the faithful are identified with their church, justification also includes the whole community of believers as the normal object of its critique. The Christian faith should play a critical role regarding human life, both in general and in particular. For humanity stands under the judgment of the Creator, who is also the final end of his creation. But the possibility that human persons can still look at God in hope in spite of their sinfulness derives precisely from the fact that the judgment of God on the world has been expressed once for all in the cross of Christ. The taking on of human sin by the Word made flesh is the basic statement of what human beings have been and continue to be. At the same time it is the source of their reconciliation with God. Justification by faith as critical principle teaches us that the divine judgment is like a two-edged sword, cutting one way against sin and the estrangement of humanity from God, and cutting the other way to establish the true righteousness based on Jesus Christ and offered to us as the source and the object of our faith and trust. Everything in the church, whether universal or local, that obscures this message falls under prophetic judgment.

It follows from this that justification by faith alone has a fourth function: it is a principle for the spiritual life. There have been many schools of so-called spirituality, some focusing attention on one of the mysteries of Christ, others on specific virtues to be practiced, some on a style of life, as in a religious order or a monastery, others on following and imitating a saint who, for example, like Francis of Assisi has been a model and an inspiration for many. Luther was particularly conscious of the dangers of such focused spiritualities, for they can in their particularity hide the central mystery of Christ. Yet he also knew that justification by faith can itself be the principle for a profound spiritual life, because one could place one's entire being under the judgment of God, seeking protection from the wrath of God in the only shelter offered to us, namely, Jesus Christ. Justification can help sort out the values and deficiencies of all systems of spiritual life, of all ascetic practices, and of all descriptions of mystical states. It reminds those who wish to live nearer to God that all callings and vocations are holy, and in all one can experience the gift of Christ's righteousness imputed to us out of love. The model for prayer is none other than the Psalms with their focus on the mercy of God for his people.

Luther indeed carried out all these applications of justification by faith; he spoke about them in his biblical commentaries, his sermons, and his many occasional writings. Should there still be another function of justification by faith? Can it also be a speculative principle on which one could build theological systems? Luther himself never used it in this way. He never built a system and he criticized the scholastic synthesis. This is not to say that no system can ever be erected on justification by faith; it would give cohesion to impressive speculation, but what such a system would look like is not apparent. The systems of thought developed by Lutheran Orthodoxy, which incorporated large doses of Scholasticism, have not been able to last. More recent Protestant systems, such as those of Schleiermacher or Paul Tillich, have considerably altered Luther's insight into justification. The danger here is that in the process of building a system of thought one may reinterpret the principle of justification in the light of the system. And then justification would lose its critical dimension; it would become a piece of a broader fabric. This it cannot be without ceasing to function as the fundamental principle for methodology, exegesis, self-criticism, and spirituality.

SIXTEENTH AND TWENTIETH CENTURIES

The major questions of the twentieth century are not at first glance close to those of the sixteenth century. Allegiance to tradition has been replaced by expectation for the future. Respect for social organization has given way to concern for social justice. Princes and natural leaders no longer dominate the common man. Scholastic theology has lost its central place in higher education, and this place is now occupied by the theoretical and applied sciences. The Christian world is no longer limited to Europe, but has become geographically universal. The threat to Christianity does not come from Turks and Muslims, but from practical atheism in the Western democracies and from theoretical and political atheism in communist countries. Present society, like modern science, governs itself "as though there were no God." At the same time economic problems dominate the horizon for both governments and individuals. The wish for comfort and efficiency makes humanity subservient to machines.

Under these conditions the major personal problem one encounters is not that of the "terrified conscience" laboring under a law too hard to be kept. It is rather that of solitude and alienation. Modern humanity, claiming to have "come of age," has lost its bearings. Detached from nature, which they want to master, people feel more and more alone. Social relationships are affected to the point that marriages break down easily, that standards of ethics disintegrate. The world and life itself seem to be meaningless to many.

It has been a constant problem for the Christian faith that it has needed to be reexpressed, reinterpreted. Some of the titles formerly given to the Savior no longer say anything to most believers. We do not commonly call Jesus "the Servant of God," though we can still understand what this suggests. One can therefore ask if justification by faith as Luther understood it can still be preached in our times. Or is it an obsolete concept that had its use in the past but may well be discarded at this time?

Because it lies at the center of Christian experience, justification by faith is not expendable. Furthermore, this insight into what the gospel means seems particularly suited to our times. For total reliance on the gift of God in Jesus Christ did not only calm the anguish of the terrified conscience of the sixteenth century, it can also fill the void within that is frequently felt today. It can bridge the gap between the ideal and the real, between essence and existence. Because it takes one out of oneself to find one's true home in the Other, the gospel as formulated by Luther can take modern people away from their "human, too human" concerns. Moreover, the righteousness that makes us just through faith is not ours. In a sense it is alien from us, not indeed with the meaning of "estranged," rather in that it does not belong to us but to the Lord Jesus Christ. In this alien righteousness modern alienation can be healed. We experience the alienation of the worker who is not the master of his work, of the manager who manages people as though they were robots, of the poor who are crushed by their impotency in the face of social evil, of the rich who find no fulfillment in wealth. The solution that the Christian faith proposes is the cross. "He who loses his life shall find it." It is only by shedding our self-reliance that we can find peace. But to shed one's self-reliance without relying on anything or anyone would bring us once again to the brink of despair. The gospel presents Jesus Christ and his cross as the sign and instrument of God's reconciling action. It calls to a new life lived not in oneself, but in Jesus Christ. It opens us up to "conversion," to turning away from our sinful selves toward the God who is Creator and Savior, the beginning and the end.

FOR STUDY AND DISCUSSION

1. What was Luther's central insight concerning the relationship of God and humankind? What did "gospel" mean for Luther? What is "the faith that justifies"? Explain the terms *faith alone, grace alone, Christ alone.*

2. Define "theology" as understood in the light of "justification by faith."

3. What is the difference between a "theologian of glory" and a "theologian of the cross"?

4. Explain the distinction between law and gospel in Luther's theology.

5. What were the three short tractates Luther composed in 1520, and what was the main point of each one?

6. According to Luther, when is the human will powerless? What is the meaning and value of the doctrine of predestination? What are some functions of the doctrine of justification? What is the meaning of justification in today's world?

For Further Reading

Reumann, John. *Righteousness in the New Testament: Justification in Lutheran-Catholic Dialogue.* Philadelphia: Fortress Press, 1982.

Forde, Gerhard. *Justification by Faith—A Matter of Death and Life.* Philadelphia: Fortress Press, 1982.

Tavard, George H. *Justification: An Ecumenical Study.* New York: Paulist Press, 1983.

4

Key Doctrines

One problem for the reader of Luther's works is his style. A preacher rather than a systematic or historical theologian, he was deeply involved in the polemics into which circumstances drew him. Because of this and because his vocabulary, whether in Latin or in German, was extensive and colorful, he often went far beyond what today would be considered civilized debate. Those who tend to agree with him without question, perhaps because they have been brought up in a Protestant tradition, should not take all his attacks at face-value. He tended to exaggerate the foibles of his opponents. On the other hand, those who tend to feel hostile about him, perhaps because they have been brought up in the Roman Catholic tradition, have to ignore many of his polemical accents in order to appreciate the positive aspects of his teachings. Furthermore, one can view Luther's theological ideas from two perspectives. In contrast to other continental reformers, such as Zwingli or Calvin, Luther is very traditional. Yet in relation to the aspects of Roman Catholicism which he criticized, he seems quite radical. The two viewpoints are inseparable.

The principle of justification by faith immediately entailed consequences concerning the sources of theology. Because of certain decisions about indulgences made by the Catholic hierarchy in Rome and in Germany, Luther had sharply reacted against the teaching on indulgences. Reflection on this pastoral problem made him perceive better some aspects of what he already knew to be the heart of the gospel, namely, justification by faith alone without works. Since his adversaries could easily argue in favor of indulgences because of medieval custom, papal decrees, and episcopal letters, he had to found his doctrine on an unimpeachable source which neither custom nor decree could nullify. This was Scripture and chiefly the New Testament, where the epistles of Paul to the Romans and the Galatians contain formulations that are basic to justification by faith. By the same token, Luther insisted on Scripture alone as the source of faith. Yet Scripture in his perspective is not to be taken in too bookish a sense. Scripture is the Word of God. It is not, as such, a book. The written New Testament is Scripture only insofar as the Word of God shines through it. This explains why Luther feels free with the written words. What binds him to Scripture is not the text as such, but the fact that the text, so to speak, shows forth Christ. In Luther's language it is *was Christus treibet* that counts. (This expression means something like "what promotes Christ," but with a more down-to-earth tone than in this English translation.) For this reason Luther did not think much of the Epistle of James. Many argued from it against his interpretation of Paul, but Luther noticed this epistle says little, if anything, of Christ himself.

Against the Catholic polemicists, moreover, Luther refused to make his reading of Scripture subservient to decisions made much later by councils, even ecumenical councils representing the whole episcopate of the church. Not that he opposed councils in principle, but he wanted councils to remain what they were or should have been, namely, witnesses to Scripture and its meaning. The notion that councils may have erred in faith was acceptable to him, for they were gatherings of churchmen, and churchmen are not free from mistakes and infidelities. Scripture alone thus became the counterpart of faith alone. It did not rule out the valuable data of later tradition any more than faith alone ruled out the good works of the faithful. But just as faith alone ensures that the faithful will not rely on their own works for salvation, Scripture alone ensures that the Word of God, as perceived in Scripture, can rule unimpeded.

Yet, in spite of what some of Luther's adversaries claimed, this emphasis on Scripture alone was not tantamount to privately interpreting the Bible. Luther knew that the faithful belong to a community and that the gospel is not addressed only to individuals in their solitude. The Word has to be preached in the context of the church and the sacraments. These three notions—church, Word, and sacrament—are closely related. The church is to be found, as Philipp Melanchthon formulated it in Article VII of the *Augsburg Confession*, "where the

Word is rightly preached, and the sacraments are rightly administered."

SACRAMENTS AND MINISTRY

Luther's theology of the sacraments is indebted both to the medieval tradition from which he came and to the central insight of justification by faith. To the medieval tradition Luther owed his belief that some ceremonies of the church go back to apostolic times, that the church is not free to alter such ceremonies substantially, and that they are to some degree constitutive of what the church is as a community or society. But where the late medieval tradition as embodied in the Council of Florence counted seven such sacraments, Luther, as we have seen, reduced this number precisely because of justification by faith alone.

His leading principle is that sacraments should express to their recipients that God is now justifying them through Christ by the power of the Holy Spirit. The words and the gestures of each sacrament are now seen as expressing neither divine grace in general nor some actual grace needed for carrying out certain responsibilities (as was the common medieval view), but only the grace of justification. On this basis Luther finds that in Scripture only two sacraments clearly express justification: baptism and the Eucharist. Because baptism is described by St. Paul as participation in the dying and rising of Christ, it is an eloquent proclamation of life out of death, of justification by faith, for it is independent of conditions on the part of the recipient and therefore is properly given to infants. Because the Eucharist is the sacrament of Christ's own gift of his body and blood, it is the other sacrament of the gospel in Luther's strict understanding of the term sacrament. As for the other five sacraments of the Catholic tradition, Luther himself practiced penance, or reconciliation, precisely because it expresses justification by faith. Yet since he did not find penance to be a sacrament clearly taught in Scripture, he would not count it a sacrament in the strict sense. In regard to confirmation, orders, healing of the sick, and marriage, Luther, who was in fact not well-versed in their history, held to the hypothesis that they were only medieval inventions connected with the human urge to rely on one's works for salvation. Therefore he saw them as based on works, not on faith.

Among the most important consequences of Luther's basic principle of justification is his alteration of the traditional eucharistic liturgy. Partly to counterbalance the excesses of Karlstadt, one of his early followers, Luther had to take steps in order to develop a smooth transition from the old liturgy, for it emphasized sacrament rather than Word, and in the minds of the people it tended to exaggerate the importance given to good works. Luther wished for a new liturgy centered on Christ alone. Such a liturgy would primarily express the gift of justification by grace through faith; the proclamation of the Word would be predominant and would itself regulate the sacramental aspect of the celebration. In this respect it was unfortunate that the age in which Luther lived was not by any standard a great liturgical period. Actually the Latin Middle Ages, unlike the Byzantine period, was quite deficient in the theology of the liturgy. There was an impressive sacramental theology in the writings of Scholastic theologians. But its application to the texts and attitudes of worship was largely left to rubrics; and the rubrics were themselves the product of canonical tradition and of the discipline of the sacraments as these had evolved step by step rather than of theological reflection on worship. The result was that in order to reformulate the Mass and to make sure that this would no longer be interpreted as a new sacrifice offered now by a priest for the sins of the people, Luther practically did away with the traditional eucharistic prayer. He replaced it with a simple reading of the account of the Last Supper.

In doing this, Luther was more medieval than he thought; to focus the Eucharist on the words of Jesus at the Last Supper was in keeping with a tradition already operative in Thomas Aquinas according to which the essence of the eucharistic liturgy lies precisely in these so-called words of consecration. A more historical view would have seen the words of consecration only as the second moment in a eucharistic liturgy which, beginning with thanksgiving to God the Father in the "preface," proceeds to tell the story of the Last Supper and culminates in invoking the Holy Spirit to come upon the gifts and upon the congregation. To fill out this shortened medieval form of the Mass, Luther and his followers developed congregational singing. In the imagination of most people it was the reform of worship which characterized the Reformation. The popular test of membership was not so much, To

58

what doctrine do you subscribe? as, What form of worship do you prefer? The first thing that the missionaries of the Reformation, whether Lutheran or Calvinist, did when they obtained the ear of the princes and magistrates was to abolish the Mass.

Be that as it may, it soon became necessary for Luther, with his understanding of the Eucharist and his new liturgy, to reinterpret the traditional priesthood. Here again Luther was less innovative than he could have been. Rejecting ordination as a sacrament in the strict sense, he identified priesthood as a prerogative accruing to all Christians through baptism. The scriptural notion of the priesthood of the people of God (1 Peter 2:5, 9; Revelation 15:10) had been derived in the Middle Ages from the belief that three sacraments (baptism, confirmation, ordination) imply, along with grace, an "indelible character" related to the high priesthood of Christ. Luther went back to scriptural formulations which he interpreted according to a more individualistic perspective. Whereas in 1 Peter it is the whole people which is priestly, in line with the individualism of the medieval interpretation, it is now each Christian who is a priest. Yet although he denied that ministerial priesthood is attached to a particular sacrament other than baptism, Luther did not wish to do away with the special responsibility of those who are ordained to minister. He fully maintained the ministry is a special order of service within the people of God. The "public office" truly belongs in the church.

THE CHURCH

Luther never wanted to start a new church. All he intended was to bring long-overdue reforms to the old church. And there were many, even on the papal side, for whom reforms were urgent. It was Luther's tragedy that the misunderstandings following the writing of the Ninety-five Theses developed into violent antagonism and irreparable separations. The early writings of the reformer are not hostile to the bishops or to the pope. In fact, when he took his stand against the doctrine of indulgences being preached in Germany, Luther fully expected to be supported by the episcopal hierarchy. For in his understanding the church is not man-made, but is the creature of God; its leaders have the responsibility of maintaining the faith once proclaimed to the saints. In particular, they have the duty of making sure that justification is properly understood and that the faithful do not fall back on themselves, replacing the undeserved righteousness that is given to us in Christ with a righteousness of their own which can only be a form of pride and self-sufficiency.

But Luther's central idea of justification by faith alone was rejected by the Roman hierarchy. Either there were too many who had too much to lose from stopping the campaign for indulgences or the theological training and assumptions of his adversaries made them impervious to his arguments. Or both! In any case Luther found himself in opposition to the hierarchy in Germany and abroad. With few exceptions, the German bishops did not follow him. The bishop of Rome, Leo X, condemned him. The universities, when they were consulted, commonly rejected his theology, except for those with which he was more personally connected and which were protected by German princes tolerant of or favorable to Luther's positions.

Under these conditions Luther had to reflect on the nature of the church of Christ. Is it an institution established by the apostles and continuing through the ages true to itself and to its founder, Jesus Christ? Is it an association of believers who come together for common purposes, such as worship, but whose responsibility for the gospel is largely individual? Luther tried to find a middle way. Neither simply an institution with guaranteed structures dispensing guidance from the Holy Spirit at all times nor a mere conglomeration of individual pieties, the church is recognizable where the Word is preached—that is, where justification by faith is recognized and proclaimed as the heart of the gospel—and the sacraments rightly administered—that is, in keeping with their purpose of effectively proclaiming justification to the faithful. In contrast with the medieval view, the church in Luther's theology seems to be discontinuous. Yet Luther does not think that the church comes and goes. As an institution it goes back to the apostles and therefore stands in some sort of apostolic succession. Yet there is no guarantee that it cannot, here and there or from time to time, be unfaithful to the gospel, for both its people and its ministers are sinful, and their sin interferes with the proper function of the church.

Unable to maintain the traditional episcopal structure because the bishops of Germany had generally sided against him, Luther had to organize the church differently, on a sort of emergency basis. Under these circumstances he came to rely on the princes and the political order since he wanted the preachers to devote all their strength to the gospel and to doctrine. What mattered was that the church give itself those structures needed to preach the gospel effectively. Thus the gospel again became the norm for church structure. Those within the church who oppose the gospel take upon themselves the features of antichrist.

A tractate of 1539, *On Councils and the Church*, gives a good view of the theological synthesis that Luther was developing on the nature of the church. This writing shows that, although Luther was not a historian, he was able to do responsible historical research. In this case he read practically all that was then available in Latin on the early councils. The result is a remarkable study in three parts. The first generally questions the authority of the church fathers and the early councils. Since these fathers are not Scripture and they have on some points contradicted one another, Luther concludes that one should study each, look carefully at his doctrines, and assess each in the light of Scripture. The second part is a painstaking study of the first four ecumenical councils with special attention to the first, the Council of Nicaea (325). Luther concludes that each taught true doctrine, but that some of their practical decisions in matters of discipline need not apply any longer. He wishes that more information were available about the circumstances of the Council of Chalcedon (451). Luther did not extend this study to the later patristic councils; but in this case he no longer trusted his historical information, which he thought came too exclusively from papal sources to be fully reliable. He reaches a series of conclusions on the authority of councils. Negatively, they cannot introduce new articles of faith, cannot command new good works, impose new ceremonies, or interfere in secular government. Positively, they are "servant and judge" at the service of God's Word for the sake of the church. Their purpose is "to confess the ancient faith" when faith is in danger. Their argumentation should entirely be molded by the Word. Luther proposes, as examples of such argumentation, "the dialectic of St. Peter, St. Paul, and St. Augustine," thus showing that he is eager to listen to the voices of the fathers of the church (Augustine, as well as Peter or Paul) when they are the faithful echo of the Word of God.

In the third part he draws some interesting conclusions about the true nature of the church. Here Luther enlarges on the two marks of the church in the *Augsburg Confession*. The true church is recognizable by "the Word of God," by the two sacraments of baptism and the Eucharist, by the public office of the keys, by its ministry, by its worship, and by the fact that it suffers persecution. Such a church, Luther concludes, "cannot fail us."

PURGATORY AND PRAYER TO THE SAINTS

This assessment of the ecumenical councils clearly indicates that Luther is not a radical, eager to espouse any novelty. His is a conservative reformation. That this is not the way it looks when seen from within Roman Catholicism may be the result of Luther's negative judgments on some aspects of medieval piety which have continued in Catholic life. For instance, the controversy over indulgences raised the question of purgatory. The Ninety-five Theses themselves did not deny purgatory. They only indicated uncertainty about its nature, and such an uncertainty was not uncommon in the theology of the period. They also proposed what purgatory can possibly mean: "There seems to be the same difference between hell, purgatory, and heaven as between despair, uncertainty, and assurance" (Thesis 16). In fact, there have been two theologies of purgatory. For some, seemingly the majority, it is a time of expiation for the penalty due to sin, when sin has been forgiven but the penalty has not been adequately paid in this life. For others it means a time of positive preparation and purification by divine grace before they see God face to face. Luther in fact never speaks of this second theology of purgatory. What he denies is the first view. He is soon led to conclude that once the doctrine of justification by faith alone has become the center of theology, there is no room for purgatory as expiation. For expiation is a human work, and salvation is neither based on nor conditioned by any human work, however well meaning and holy. Applying what is called Occam's razor (that is, the principle formulated by John Duns Scotus at the end of the thirteenth century that "entities are not to be multiplied needlessly"),

Luther concludes that purgatory is not necessary. Justification by grace through faith is not only the first but also the final word about salvation. The righteousness of Christ imputed to sinners by God is the sole means of salvation. Therefore purgatory, as Luther understands it, is a superfluous entity. Furthermore, it has no direct basis in Scripture, since the clearest text that can be quoted for it is from 2 Maccabees 12:38–45, and the exact status of this book in the canon of the Old Testament was not settled in Catholic theology itself. Luther generally had opted for the Hebrew canon of Jerusalem instead of the larger Greek canon of Alexandria (the Septuagint), which was the model for the Latin Vulgate. The so-called Apocrypha of the Old Testament were thereby excluded from normative Scripture, though they were still frequently used for reading and edification.

Just as purgatory disappears from Luther's theology because it seems to have lost its purpose, the invocation of saints also vanishes. For prayer to the saints is closely related to the idea that during their lives the saints acquired merits which when added to the merits of Christ are available to sinners to rely upon. Thus Luther held that prayer to the saints favors reliance on works rather than on the right-eousness of Christ imputed to us by God out of pure love. This was one of the ideas behind the practice of indulgences. By the same token he considered the idea that saints can intervene from heaven on our behalf to contradict the scriptural teaching that Jesus Christ is the only mediator of salvation.

MOTHER OF GOD

With respect to the Virgin Mary, however, Luther was not as negative as later Protestantism generally became. In fact, in 1521 he composed a beautiful commentary on Mary's song, the *Magnificat*. Along with the patristic and medieval traditions, he recognizes her perpetual virginity and he duly acknowledges that she is properly called the "Mother of God"; this title sums up all that she has received from God. "Men have crowded her glory into a single word, calling her the Mother of God. No one can say anything greater of her or to her. . . ." This is indeed an unfathomable dignity worthy of contemplation. "It needs to be pondered in the heart what it means to be the Mother of God." Luther does not mention the immaculate conception (which was not yet unanimously accepted among Catholic theologians) or the assumption. And he warns against excesses in Marian piety; those who want to give her "proper honor must not regard her alone and by herself," for her true honor lies in her low estate as the servant of Christ. This commentary goes on to show that Mary is a marvelous example of faith, that in her one sees the grace of God at work, and that all her life consists in praising God for his deeds. Luther identifies six such deeds as described in six verses of the *Magnificat*. In passing he criticizes artists who paint Mary in such a lofty way that she is given false glory. Queen of heaven she is, but not a goddess. True devotion consists in "blessing her," that is, in giving God all the glory that one finds in her because God put it there.

Reading Luther's *Magnificat* helps us understand the piety he practiced. From his concept of faith as trust and assurance, or from the explanations of the Creed in Luther's two catechisms (in which the articles of the Creed are personalized so that they are reformulated in relation to "me," *pro me*), one could get the impression that Luther practices a self-centered piety or that he understands the gospel chiefly in terms of what God does "for me." Personal warmth corresponds indeed to one aspect of his spirituality. But the *Magnificat* emphasizes another aspect of his spirituality; it is in lowliness that God is truly praised; the works of God are within; God himself is a hidden God (*Deus absconditus*, as Luther expresses it in many of his works), and such a God, who can only be praised from afar, can only be worshiped, adored, and contemplated. The *Magnificat* constitutes an invitation to contemplation in the best tradition of Rhineland mysticism. The deepest contemplation is reserved for what, at the beginning of the *Smalcald Articles*, Luther calls "the high articles of the majesty of God," namely, the Trinity and the incarnation, concerning which, he states, "there is no controversy between us and our adversaries."

REDEMPTION, INCARNATION, TRINITY

The polemics of the period induced Luther to speak mostly of redemption because it is the immediate source of grace and justification. Redemption sums up the purpose of the incarnation and is the revealing event through which we know God as three persons. Luther's view of redemption was deeply indebted to St. Anselm of Canterbury (1033–1109), who explained redemption as satisfaction made on our behalf by the only one who could adequately satisfy divine righteousness, namely, the Lord incarnate. In some of his more popular passages Luther also used patristic and medieval images in which Christ was compared to a fighter dealing the knock-out blow to our adversary the devil and thereby freeing us from his clutches. Behind such imagery there is, along with the desire to speak to simple people in vivid fashion, the conviction that Jesus Christ redeems us through the reality of his flesh and blood, not by an abstract principle of righteousness but by taking upon himself our daily struggle with the forces of evil. In his biblical commentaries Luther also wrote extensively on the incarnation. He favored a "high" Christology, one closely related to that of St. Cyril of Alexandria. In contrast to a "low" Christology that focuses on the humanity of Jesus, a high Christology starts from the divinity of the Word of God. Thus even when describing the humility of the human condition of Jesus and his humiliation at the cross, Luther is emphatic that this is indeed the Word of God. He insists upon the "interchange of qualities" between the divine and the human in Christ, seeing the humanity of Jesus as the medium of the divine Word. This humanity shares the qualities of the divinity, yet in the humble condition of the suffering Servant of God. Luther even carried this to an extreme, as when in controversies about the real presence in the Eucharist, he claimed that the risen body of Christ is everywhere present.

The doctrine of the Trinity was also of major importance to Luther. His works contain suggestive formulas which show that he had reflected deeply on this fundamental divine mystery. Thus in his commentary of 1519 on Galatians 4:6, Luther says: "Likewise we are, we are moved, and we live in God: we are, on account of the Father who is the substance of the Divinity; we are moved by the image of the Son who is born of the Father, as it were, in a divine and eternal movement; we live according to the Spirit in whom the Father and the Son rest and, as it were, live."

LETTING FAITH TRANSFORM VISION

Again, one may ask: Is this application of Luther's central insight of justification by faith to the broader aspects of his theology relevant to the concerns of Christians in the twentieth century?

The answer is really quite simple. If Christians are now interested only in the process by which they can transform the world, then Luther is not relevant. For such a process, whether by violent revolution or by progressive betterment, depends on human plans based on economic analysis, political theory, and sociological realities; it relates both to the imaginative construction of utopias and to the realistic implementation of new societal structures. But all this rests on human reason and its capacities, on the human will and its ambitions.

If, however, Christians can look beyond this horizon in two directions—toward the personal self and toward the wider universe—then the answer is different. Psychological introspection, which is recommended today by so many spiritual or pseudoreligious movements, soon leads to the limitations of one's own self-centeredness. And there is no better remedy for these limitations than by going beyond oneself through justification by faith alone. For then one trusts not in oneself, but in the Lord. Once apprehended, this going beyond oneself through the righteousness of Jesus Christ is bound to penetrate all dimensions of thought and of life, including the social dimension. It becomes a principle which transforms one's entire life, affecting all church doctrines and changing the tone of all philosophies and all human sciences. The way in which such a tranformation took place in Luther's own thought need not be a model for everyone to follow. Yet it does help to gauge the all-encompassing character of the righteousness of Christ.

The wider universe is an unimaginable conglomerate of billions of galaxies, each containing billions of solar systems. It both dwarfs us and exalts us. It makes us know our littleness, yet it opens before us inexhaustible possibilities for the future. How can we really function in such a universe unless it is not on ourselves that we really count, but on the Creator? Luther was eager that faith should transform his whole world. If the world seems to us immensely larger than his, there is all the more urgency for letting faith transform our vision.

FOR STUDY AND DISCUSSION

1. What are specific problems of which one should be aware when reading Luther's works? What did Luther mean by "Scripture alone"?

2. What was Luther's understanding of the sacraments in contrast to the Roman Catholic understanding? How did Luther reinterpret the traditional priesthood in the light of his understanding of the Eucharist and his new liturgy?

3. What was Luther's view of the nature of the church, and how did he think the church should be structured?

4. Explain Luther's judgment regarding the medieval view of purgatory and the invocation of saints. Also explain his views regarding the Virgin Mary, redemption, the incarnation, and the Trinity.

5. What kind of transforming vision of the world derived from Luther's central theological insight? Is it possible for all Christians today to have a similar transforming vision?

For Further Reading

Althaus, Paul. *The Theology of Martin Luther*. Philadelphia: Fortress Press, 1966.

McSorley, Harry. *Luther: Right or Wrong? An Ecumenical-Theological Study of Luther's Major Work, The Bondage of the Will*. Minneapolis: Augsburg Publishing House, 1969.

5

The Rough Woodsman

By his own admission Martin Luther was an angry man. Anger was his special sin. But anger could also be necessary and proper. It helped him, he said, to write well, to pray, and to preach. "Anger refreshes all my blood, sharpens my mind, and drives away temptations," he once commented. He was aware that some were offended by his harshness and anger. But he had an explanation: "I was born to war with fanatics and devils," he wrote in 1529. "Thus my books are very stormy and bellicose. I must root out the stumps and trunks, hew away the thorns and briar, fill in the puddles. I am the rough woodsman, who must pioneer and hew a path."

There is much truth to this excuse. Luther was a pioneer who used his angry pen to blaze a new path for others to follow. Even so, we today are often put off by the angry self-righteousness, the intolerance, the vulgarity, and the violence of Luther's attacks on others. "Can these be the works of a truly religious man?" we ask. The question is not new. The moderate Catholic, Duke George of Saxony, in his reply to one of Luther's more pungent attacks challenged Luther's supporters: "Now with what insidious perfidy, lies, screams, and bawling [Luther attacks the Catholics] and how often he used the devil's name besides, I shall let others, who are always saying that he is a holy man and possesses the Holy Spirit, offer some explanation." Melanchthon's words, spoken at Luther's funeral, illustrate one contemporary Protestant reply to this challenge:

> Some by no means evil-minded persons have complained that Luther displayed too much severity. I will not deny this. But I answer in the language of Erasmus: "Because of the magnitude of the disorders God gave this age a violent physician."

For Catholics Luther's harshness constituted persuasive evidence that

Luther was no man of God. For Protestants Luther's harshness was a necessary response to the spiritual conditions of the age. Obviously with such disagreement we must examine the background and significance of Luther's attacks before we pass judgment on them.

THE DEVIL AND THE END TIME

Once Luther had identified the papacy as the prophesied antichrist seated within the church (see chapter 2), he concluded that he must be living on the eve of the Last Judgment. The final battle had been joined. Satan would unleash all his servants in a last, desperate attempt to defeat the servants of Christ. Luther must prepare to do his part in this final struggle. As the years passed and Luther faced new opponents, he viewed them in terms of this final battle. This requires some further explanation.

Luther placed his conflicts into a larger Augustinian view of the dynamics of history, a view which had been the common property of Western Christendom for a thousand years. Early in his career as a reformer, his reading of the Bible convinced Luther that practically from the beginning of the world there had been a perpetual, unchanging struggle between the true and false church. He saw this struggle as involving a recurrent contest between true and false prophets and apostles. Believing that mankind did not change and that the devil never slept, he could trace this struggle from the biblical histories into his own time. What happened to the prophets and apostles in their day could and would happen to the church of his day. Their experiences established a paradigm of the dynamics of all sacred history.

Within this paradigm the papacy was the antichrist described in Scripture. As Luther encountered additional opponents through the years, he integrated them into the paradigm. Opponents within Protestantism were deemed contemporary false prophets and apostles, like those who had plagued the true prophets and apostles. The Turks were identified with Gog and the little horn in the Book of Daniel. And contemporary Jewry was seen as the remnant of a rejected people suffering under God's wrath for their rejection of the true Messiah. They were all members of the false church. Luther understood his disagreements with them in the context of this struggle between God and Satan. And behind them all loomed the figure of the devil, the

70

father of lies. Often Luther directed his attacks not at his human opponents but at the devil whom he saw as their master, and, of course, no language was too harsh when attacking the devil.

Since Luther was always drawing comparisons and parallels between these opponents and the opponents of the prophets and apostles, it was only natural that he would see the true prophets and apostles as having provided a precedent for the way in which one should deal with such opponents. As a result he could explain and justify his polemics and his stubbornness on points of doctrine by pointing to the example set by these men of God. When, for example, he rebuked his age for its failings, it was a prophet like Jeremiah from whom he borrowed his style, his tone, often the language itself. When he blasted the papacy as a wanton whore, he was borrowing language from Hosea and Ezekiel. His great comfort was Paul, who taught that "if . . . an angel from heaven should preach to you a gospel contrary to that which we preached to you, let him be accursed" (Galatians 1:8).

Luther's many attacks cannot be fully understood apart from this context, as strange as it may seem to us today. The self-righteousness, the vulgarity, and the violence owe much to Luther's intense conviction that he was engaged in the climactic battle between the true and false church, that the real opponents were not men but devils, and the stakes were salvation and eternal life.

THE FALSE BRETHREN

Luther first encountered opponents within the Protestant ranks in 1522, when he was called home from the Wartburg by members of his Wittenberg congregation to deal with a reform movement that some felt had gotten out of hand. Although the leaders of this movement, his colleague Andreas Bodenstein von Karlstadt and a fellow Augustinian, Gabriel Zwilling, were instituting reforms that Luther himself had advocated in his writings, they were doing so with such haste and disregard for both political realities and the sensibilities of sincere Christians that Luther felt it necessary to intervene. On March 9, 1522, tonsured and garbed once again as an Augustinian, Luther mounted the pulpit of the Wittenberg parish church to begin the famous "Invocavit" sermons that reestablished his control over the progress of the Reformation in Wittenberg. "The cause is good," he told his congregation, "but there has been too much haste. For there are still brothers and sisters on the other side who belong to us and must still be won."

As for Karlstadt and Zwilling and three laymen, the so-called Zwickau prophets who claimed direct revelation, Luther charged that Satan had once again sent his false prophets to mislead the true church. Clear evidence for the satanic motivation of these men, he believed, was their insistence that people were guilty of a sin if certain Old Testament commandments and New Testament examples were not followed to the letter. Such insistence imposed the secular kingdom upon the spiritual and reshackled consciences with laws and regulations, while Christ freed them. Satan was attempting to ruin the gospel by making nonessential issues a burden to consciences.

Within weeks of his return Luther had easily overcome his first Protestant opponents and in so doing had set the pattern he was to follow in the decades ahead. He saw Satan's spirit at work in these opponents, attempting to accomplish through guile that which it had been unable to accomplish through force, and he identified many of this spirit's distinguishing characteristics. In the years ahead the actual behavior and beliefs of his Protestant opponents, his "fanatics," tended to disappear behind this vision of the false prophet, the minion of Satan.

Karlstadt and Luther never reconciled. By 1523 Karlstadt had left Wittenberg for a country parish where he undertook reforms as he saw fit. He also continued to publish treatises. Luther and the Wittenberg faculty lodged protests, Luther clashed with Karlstadt on Karlstadt's home turf, and, finally, the Saxon rulers expelled Karlstadt from Saxony.

The conflict between Luther and Karlstadt became public knowledge beyond the borders of Electoral Saxony in the autumn of 1524, following Karlstadt's expulsion and the publication of several of his attacks on Luther. Especially noted were his attacks on Luther's belief in the real presence of Christ's body and blood in the bread and wine of the Lord's Supper. Luther soon published a two-part reply, *Against the Heavenly Prophets*. In this treatise he took deadly aim at Karlstadt and his opinions. It is apparent from the outset, however, that he had more than Karlstadt in his sights. Standing behind Karlstadt was the prince of the world, Satan. As Luther attacked Karlstadt, he intended to strike Satan as well and to thwart his plan to overthrow the gospel. This metaphysical dimension of the struggle between Luther and Karlstadt influenced all of Luther's arguments and characterizations and allowed him to paint the controversy solely in blacks and whites.

The treatise was directed, moreover, at all the fanatics and false prophets, not just Karlstadt. Although much of the treatise dealt directly with Karlstadt, it was actually Karlstadt's *spirit* (which, Luther maintained, was the same spirit driving Müntzer, the Zwickau prophets, and the other "heavenly prophets") that bore the brunt of Luther's attack. And Karlstadt was faulted not only for what he had allegedly done but also for what his spirit was allegedly capable of doing, given the opportunity. Although hardly fair to Karlstadt, this approach made for a devastating attack.

THE PEASANTS' REVOLT

Luther soon saw Satan at work in another quarter. In the spring of 1525 peasant unrest spread from southern Germany northward, and Thomas Müntzer, a former Lutheran, emerged as its leader in Thuringia. In southern Germany there appeared the *Twelve Articles*, the most widely circulated peasant manifesto, which called for religious, social, and economic reform and which buttressed its demands with citations from Scripture

Eager to correct what he saw as a misunderstanding of the gospel and to disclaim responsibility for the unrest, Luther penned his *Admonition to Peace,* in which he replied to the *Twelve Articles.* In the first section, addressed to the princes and rulers, he blamed the unrest on their persecution of the gospel and their mistreatment of their subjects. Some of the articles were eminently just, and the princes should, for the sake of peace, accommodate the peasants. In the second section, addressed to the peasants, he told the peasants that their rebellion violated the gospel and both Christian and natural law. Moreover, they were blaspheming the name of Christ by quoting the gospel to justify secular demands. In fact, the gospel taught obedience to secular authorities and the suffering of injustice. Their recourse to the sword betrayed a lack of faith in God. Finally, in the third section, he admonished both the rulers and the peasants that there was nothing Christian on either side. If they came to blows, it was their responsibility, not his or the gospel's.

The treatise seems to have had little calming effect. The unrest spread. Luther personally experienced heckling and disturbances during several excursions into the Thuringian countryside and even felt his life threatened. Events swung him over to the side of the princes. In May he wrote out his uncompromising *Against the Robbing and Murdering Hordes of Peasants.* This treatise was first published in one volume with the *Admonition to Peace* under the title *Admonition to Peace and Also Against the Robbing and Murdering Hordes of the Other Peasants,* Luther's intention being that the *Admonition* was directed to the "good" peasants and the *Against the Robbing and Murdering Hordes* to the "bad" peasants. Printers quickly split the two treatises, however, and the harsher *Against the Robbing and Murdering Hordes* soon found wide circulation on its own.

Since Luther had concluded that the peasants were doing the devil's work and particularly the work of that "archdevil," Thomas Müntzer, he felt that it was his responsibility to show the peasants their error and to advise the rulers how to proceed. The peasants had violated their oaths of obedience to their rulers, oaths confirmed by Christ and St. Paul. They were in open rebellion. And they cloaked their service to the devil under the name of the gospel. To the rulers Luther offered sanguine advice. Justice was on the rulers' side. Everyone who could was to smite, slay, and stab, secretly or publicly, for nothing was more poisonous, harmful, or devilish than a rebel. The end of the world was imminent. No devil was left in hell; they had all gone into the peasants.

The uprising was brutally suppressed by the princes. Müntzer was captured, interrogated under torture, and executed. Although the revolt was over, the question of Luther's role in it remained controversial. Catholics held him and the Reformation responsible for the unrest and argued that his attacks on the peasants had been hypocritical. And even friends and supporters were offended by the violence of his attack on the peasants. But Luther felt vindicated in his judgment on the "rebellious spirit." As he saw it, this spirit had driven Müntzer into rebellion and earned him a violent death at the hands of the authorities. It had prompted the war itself, as Luther had anticipated. It had led Karlstadt into contempt for authority and an attack on the Lord's Supper. Caught up in the Peasants' Revolt, Karlstadt had been forced to seek refuge in Luther's own house and beg for Luther's forgiveness and assistance. When it was all over, Luther felt more strongly than ever that it was Satan who was behind all his Protestant opponents.

THE SACRAMENTARIANS

From the outset of the controversy with Ulrich Zwingli, reformer of Zurich, and John Oecolampadius, reformer of Basel, Luther believed that they were simply following Karlstadt when they denied that Christ's body and blood were physically present in the Lord's Supper. This belief shaped much of the controversy that followed, for it led Luther to attribute the same satanic spirit to these new opponents that he had previously attributed to Karlstadt, Müntzer, and the Zwickau prophets. His opponents, naturally enough, did not appreciate this, and they complained of it repeatedly in the exchanges that followed.

It is not surprising for Luther to conclude that Zwingli and Oecolampadius were simply following Karlstadt, although in fact their beliefs had been reached independently of Karlstadt and rested frequently on different reasoning. Although they advanced slightly different arguments to support their positions, Zwingli and Oecolampadius were in substantial agreement in denying Christ's physical presence in the elements of the Lord's Supper. Specifically, they denied that Christ's body and blood were or even could be literally and physically present in the elements either through the transformation of the substance of bread and wine (the Catholic doctrine of transubstantiation), or by "coexistence" in and under the bread and wine (Luther's belief). They argued that the words spoken by Christ at the Last Supper ("Take, eat; this is my body which is given for you. Do this in memory of me.") must be taken symbolically, the words "This is my body" meaning "This represents my body" or "This is the sign of my body." They did acknowledge a real *spiritual* presence; Christ was truly present through and in the faith of the participants in the Supper. Hence they could even speak of a spiritual eating by faith, which was faith in Christ's act of redemption. But this presence was not tied to the elements, and it depended upon and was mediated by the faith of the communicants.

For his part, Luther was convinced that the words of institution were to be understood literally, and he challenged his opponents to prove that they must be understood figuratively. As he interpreted the controversy, his opponents' two basic arguments were that Christ's ascension to heaven to sit at the right hand of God removed him physically from the world and that John 6:63 ("The flesh is of no avail") made his physical presence unnecessary. Luther attacked the first argument by attacking reason. Reason, he said, cannot prove or disprove any matter of faith. God's right hand refers not to some physical location in heaven but to God's almighty power, which at one and the same time was nowhere and yet everywhere.

This presence was not a circumscribed or local presence, but an essential presence that creates and preserves all things. Moreover, there was a special presence in the Lord's Supper, he argued, for there God was present *for you* and bound his presence through the Word. As for the argument from John 6:63, Luther insisted that this could not apply to Christ's flesh without simultaneously negating the incarnation. His opponents, he contended, misconstrued the words "spirit" and "flesh" as presented by the Bible. There were spiritual and fleshly acts, but not spiritual and fleshly things. The sacrament was a visible embodiment of God's promise of salvation through Christ. To call Christ's words into question here was to deny the promise of Christ. For Luther the essence of the gospel, God's promise of justification through faith in Christ's sacrifice, was at issue in this dispute. He could no more accept his opponent's position than he could deny the doctrine of justification by faith alone.

The dispute, between Luther and his supporters on the one side, and Zwingli, Oecolampadius, Martin Bucer of Strasbourg, and other Swiss and south Germans on the other, raged for several years. The controversy was made particularly acerbic by Luther's charge that all his opponents were possessed by Satan's spirit and were bent on destroying the true church. To us today this may seem an extremely harsh and self-righteous charge, but for Luther the controversy touched the heart of the gospel. His opponents could not possibly possess the Holy Spirit and be in error on this central issue. Lacking the Holy Spirit, they were of necessity slaves of Satan, all their avowals of Christian belief were a sham, and all evidence to the contrary could be dismissed as deception and works-righteousness.

Eventually Bucer and the south Germans were able to reach an agreement with Luther and return to the Lutheran fold. Zwingli and Oecolampadius, however, remained firm in their convictions. The

Reformed church, of which Calvin was the most prominent leader in the second generation, looks to them as founders.

THE JEWS

When Martin Luther began lecturing on the Psalms at the University of Wittenberg in 1513, those Jews left in the empire were clinging to survival in small territories often controlled by a bishop or abbot. The large territories and most of the imperial cities had expelled their Jews some years earlier. Only on rare occasions did Luther encounter Jews; he never lived in close proximity to them, but he inherited a tradition, both theological and popular, of hostility toward them. He lived within a larger community, Western Christendom, which saw the Jews as a rejected people, guilty of the murder of Christ and capable of murdering Christian children for their own evil purposes. And he lived within a local community that had expelled its Jews some ninety years earlier. Despite this heritage of suspicion and hostility, Luther's first treatise on the Jews advocated that they be treated in a friendly manner and denounced the treatment they were currently subjected to.

In 1523 Luther published *That Jesus Christ Was Born a Jew*. The treatise was occasioned by the report that Duke Ferdinand had charged that Luther denied Mary's virginity before and after Christ's birth. However, the treatise went beyond a simple refutation of these charges to explain the reasons from Scripture that induced Luther "to believe that Christ was a Jew born of a virgin." With this Luther had hoped that he might "entice some Jews to the Christian faith." Perhaps if the Jews were dealt with in a friendly fashion and were instructed carefully from the Holy Scripture, "many of them would become true Christians and would return to the faith of their fathers, the prophets and patriarchs." To reject their beliefs so absolutely, allowing nothing to remain, and to treat them solely with arrogance and scorn, may frighten them away from true Christianity.

Luther closed with a remarkable appeal to his fellow Christians:

> Therefore, I would request and advise that one manage them decently and instruct them from the Scripture so that some of them might be brought along. But since we now drive them with force and slander them, accuse them of having Christian blood if they don't stink, and who knows what other foolishness, so that they are regarded just as dogs—what good

77

can we expect to accomplish with them? Similarly, that we forbid them to work, do business, and have other human association with us, so that we drive them to usury—how does that help them?

If we wish to help them, we must practice on them not the papal law but rather the Christian law of love, and accept them in a friendly fashion, allowing them to work and make a living, so that they gain the reason and opportunity to be with and among us [and] to see and to hear our Christian teaching and life. If some are obstinate, what does it matter? After all, we too are not all good Christians. Here I will let matters rest until I see what I have accomplished.

The missionary tendency of this treatise is apparent. Although Luther firmly believed that the conversion of the Jews rests solely in God's hands, he appears to have had some hope that by exposing them to the true gospel, unadulterated by papal additions, an appreciable number of Jews might convert. While the renewed gospel was given time to do its work, patience and tolerance was to be shown the Jews.

Although Luther had relatively little to say about the Jews during the late 1520s and the early 1530s, there is evidence that sometime before 1536 three learned Jews had visited him and, on the basis of their rabbinic tradition, had taken issue with the interpretation Luther placed on various messianic passages in the Old Testament. Already disappointed with the meager success of his earlier missionary efforts, Luther was so frustrated by this conversation that he vowed not to enter into such a dialog again. But this issue, the proper interpretation of messianic passages in the Old Testament, remained much on his mind during his final years and found violent expression in his notorious attacks of 1543, especially his *On the Jews and Their Lies*.

The primary target of these treatises is rabbinic exegesis. For Luther a christocentric reading of the Old Testament or Hebrew Bible was crucial. He believed that the true church of God had been established even before the Fall when God commanded Adam to eat from every tree except the tree of the knowledge of good and evil. When Satan had tempted Adam and Eve and they had fallen, God had immediately announced the promise of the blessed seed that would crush the head of the serpent. The saints of the Old Testament or Hebrew Bible lived and taught this faith in the promise of the seed of the woman. "They gave the exact same sermons that we in our time present to the church and community of God, except that they taught about the future Christ who was yet to come, but we say of him: 'Christ has come,' while they said: 'He will come.'" For this reason Luther interpreted the Old Testament or Hebrew Bible christologically and saw all promises by God in the Old Testament or Hebrew Bible as referring to Christ. Following medieval exegesis, he further believed that the Old Testament or Hebrew Bible testified not only to Christ but to the Trinity as well.

Rabbinic exegesis challenged both views. And under the influence of humanist scholarship, which placed a premium on going to the sources and on applying historical and philological techniques to the sources, Protestant theologians and exegetes were adopting the more historical and source-critical exegetical opinions of Jewish exegetes.

The bulk of Luther's anti-Jewish treatises consists of an elaborate attempt to dissuade fellow Protestants from employing rabbinic exegesis. He attacked the exegesis itself, using historical, scriptural, and theological arguments. But he also employed his rhetorical skills to attack its source: the Jews themselves. To discredit the message it helps also to discredit the messenger.

Not surprisingly the lengthy exegetical passages and the christological arguments have been long forgotten, superceded by improvements in biblical scholarship, while the hostile recommendations for the treatment of the Jews have survived in fragmented form in the memories and writings of anti-Semites. Their favorite source has been the third section of *On the Jews and Their Lies*, in which Luther dealt with alleged Jewish slanders against the Virgin Mary and her son, Jesus. In this section he stated that the Jews labeled Jesus a magician and instrument of the devil. They changed Jesus' name into an insult and perverted the conventional Jewish greeting into a curse on Christians. They called Jesus a whore's son and Mary a whore, although they knew better. They claimed that Mary had conceived while menstruating, which meant that her offspring, Jesus, was insane or a demon's child, and they perverted Mary's name into the word for manure pile. Luther recounted, without unequivocally accepting as true, some of the crudest charges traditionally lodged against the Jews: that they poisoned wells and that they kidnapped children, pierced them with nails, and hacked them into pieces. He believed them guilty in thought and deed of shedding the blood of the Messiah and his Christians.

From this list of indictments Luther swung immediately into a series of harsh recommendations to secular authorities on how to deal with the Jews. Their synagogues and schools should be burned and whatever would not burn should be buried. Their homes should be destroyed. All their prayer books and Talmudic writings should be taken from them. Their rabbis should be forbidden to teach. Their safeconducts on highways should be revoked. Their usury should be forbidden and their money taken from them, although some amount could be returned to converts to Christianity so that they might support themselves. They should be put to work in the fields so that they earned their living by the sweat of their brows. Better yet, they should be expelled after a portion of their wealth had been confiscated. It was the duty of the secular authorities, Luther insisted, to implement these recommendations. It was the duty of the ecclesiastical authorities to warn and instruct their congregations about the Jews and their lies.

It would be tempting to dismiss these writings as aberrations, as medieval remnants, or as the consequences of old age. But we cannot do this. The anti-Jewish writings must be taken seriously as an accurate expression of Luther's views and as an integral part of his own theological understanding.

But this does not mean we must accept his position. On the contrary, few Lutherans or Catholics would today share Luther's apocalyptic vision of the struggle between the true and false churches. This does not mean that no serious person sees satanic forces in the world. The Holocaust, to cite a terribly relevant example, has made the reality of evil all too horribly plain. But few Christians today see Satan looming behind all those with whom they have a theological or religious disagreement. And although the threat of nuclear war can generate fears that we could be living in the end time, it is generally the fringe groups within Christianity who expect an imminent apocalypse. It is really the extremists who, believing they are soldiers of the light in the final battle of Armageddon, feel justified in attacking and abusing Jews. Modern anti-Semitism does not normally take this religious form, but rather is fueled by political ideology, nationalism, or racism.

There remains, however, the root cause of Luther's anti-Jewish opinions, and there seems no way to relativize or historicize this fundamental conviction, for it lies in Christianity itself. Luther makes much of the distinction between law and gospel, between those who are slaves to sin and those who are set free by grace. Of course, this distinction is not original with Luther. It is Pauline in inspiration. But its effect, throughout the history of Christian-Jewish relations, is to consign the Jewish religion to the status of a "has-been." Judaism is seen as a religion of "law" that has now been superceded by a religion of grace revealed through Christ.

This dichotomy may be insurmountable, for it cuts both ways. If one believes that Christ is the true Messiah who established a new covenant between God and Israel, where does this leave those who hold to the original covenant? On the other hand, if one believes that the ancient covenant between God and Israel was not transformed by the man Jesus, where does this leave those who hold to the new covenant? Christianity was born out of, but also in opposition to, Judaism.

Luther, with what for today is certainly unconscionable violence and abusiveness, points nevertheless to this fundamental and all-too-real opposition. We may overcome the prejudices and hatreds of the sixteenth century, but we still must resolve, or at least learn peacefully and tolerantly to live with, this disagreement.

LUTHER AND LUTHERANISM

When Luther attacked Catholics, other Protestants, Turks, and Jews, he attacked with all the vehemence and rhetorical skill at his command. He believed that his opponents were all minions of Satan engaged in the final, apocalyptic struggle at the dawn of the end time. We shall fail to understand Luther if we fail to remember that all his writings were conditioned by this fundamental, yet to us quite alien, conviction.

Catholics and Protestants and Jews now live in another age. We still disagree on significant issues. But we are more willing to recognize the brother and sister in each other. We are also mindful of the great injury we have done each other in the zealous pursuit of a claimed exclusive truth. We have not surrendered our convictions, but we assert them differently than Luther once did. When we turn our gaze on Luther, we recognize that he was a man conditioned by history as every man is. There is much we can learn from him, but there is also much that has no place in our modern world.

FOR STUDY AND DISCUSSION

1. In what ways is the term "rough woodsman" an appropriate description of Luther? In what context should Luther's rather intolerant attacks on others be understood? How did Luther view his opponents?

2. What kind of opposition did Luther encounter within the Protestant ranks, and how did he deal with that opposition?

3. What caused the Peasants' Revolt, and how did Luther respond to this difficult and disquieting development?

4. What was the nature of Luther's controversy with Ulrich Zwingli and John Oecolampadius? What did Luther believe about Christ's presence in the Sacrament of Holy Communion (the Mass)?

5. What was the situation of Jews in Europe at the time of the Reformation? How did Luther originally recommend that the Jews be treated? What caused a change in Luther's view of the Jews? How should his later hostile recommendations for the treatment of the Jews be understood?

6. What must one keep in mind about Luther and his writings in order to understand properly his attacks on Catholics, other Protestants, Turks, and Jews? Is Luther's approach to those who disagreed with him still appropriate in the modern world?

For Further Reading

Edwards, Mark. *Luther and the False Brethren*. Stanford, Calif.: Stanford University Press, 1975.

——. *Luther's Last Battles: Politics and Polemics, 1531–46*. Ithaca, N.Y.: Cornell University Press, 1983.

Erikson, Erik. *Young Man Luther: A Study in Psychoanalysis and History*. New York: Norton, 1958.

Hendrix, Scott. *Luther and the Papacy: Stages in a Reformation Conflict*. Philadelphia: Fortress Press, 1981.

Johnson, Roger, ed. *Psychohistory and Religion: The Case of Young Man Luther*. Philadelphia: Fortress Press, 1977.

Oberman, Heiko. *The Roots of Anti-Semitism: In the Age of Renaissance and Reformation*. Philadelphia: Fortress Press, 1983.

6

Luther's Influence

Luther's great influence is undoubtedly due to his message, to the force of his personality, and to the circumstances which pushed him into the forefront. In the same circumstances a weaker man would not have had the sort of impact that Luther had. In other circumstances his reforming voice and his message might not have been heard far and wide. As things have turned out, the influence of Luther has been so deep and so extensive that one cannot do justice to it in a short treatment. All that one can do is indicate some major points that will help assess his real importance.

VIEW OF THE WORLD

Some authors have claimed to detect Luther's mark on the very shape of the modern world. It has been held, for instance, that Luther made it impossible for the classical, static view of the world to continue to be held among the educated. Instead of a world of being in which things and persons have their set place from which they do not move, Luther introduced a world in motion. The present life, he stated, "is not a being but a becoming, not a rest but the exercise of activity; nothing is already finished and consummated, but everything moves and advances." This is much closer to the contemporary sense of process, evolution, and progress than to a Platonic world of essences or to an Aristotelian world in which everything is regulated by reason. Motion, passage, and progress were for Luther of the essence of life in the Spirit. "Do not imagine," he wrote in his 1519 commentary on Galatians 4:5, "that the life of a Christian is peace and quiet, but rather it is a process and a progress from vices to virtue, from clarity to clarity, from virtue to virtue, and the one who is not in process should not think that he is a Christian. . . ." This is of course rooted in Luther's sense of the change from death to life which takes place by faith when our sinful humanity finds itself overshadowed by the holiness of Jesus Christ. Once this is applied to the world at large, it opens a strikingly modern view of existence.

For such reasons and on the basis of similar passages elsewhere in his works, Luther has been acclaimed by some as the father of the modern world. Admittedly, the humanism of the Renaissance was on the scene before him, and other reformers such as Zwingli and Calvin were in fact closer to the Renaissance than he himself was. Yet Luther went beyond the Renaissance and its elitism in his efforts to transform the religion of the masses. He influenced a whole people with his sense of the constant transformation of things. Thus the evolutionary conception of reality which one associates with Hegel (thesis, antithesis, synthesis) really derives from Luther. And if this is the case, then the entire Marxist movement and its revolutionary impact on the present world has also come from Luther, since Marxism in its basic conception is Hegel's philosophy transposed into material categories.

The problem with this sort of overall assessment of Luther is that other claims have been made which point in the opposite direction. It has been held, for instance, that through his criticism of the church of his time, Luther dealt a death blow to the collectivism of the Middle Ages and to the corporate, organic sense of the church which prevailed before him. He is accused of being the initiator of individualism, for he set up the individual against both pope and emperor, the private reading of the Bible against authoritative interpretations by the powers that be, and the right to choose one's religion against all dogmatisms. He would thus be the source of the philosophy of the Enlightenment with its insistence on the rights of the individual. Through the French Revolution with its "rights of the human being and citizen," Luther would be the father of democracy, of liberal political systems, and of their counterpart in the economic order, liberal capitalism.

From a different perspective Luther has been seen as the initiator of modern nationalism. His sense of the German nation, his roots in the peasantry, his closeness to ordinary folk, his occasional coarseness of language, and his diatribes against the Italian character of the Roman Curia and the Italianization of the church point to him as at least a major force in the rise of nationalism. His vocal anti-Semitism has been hailed by modern anti-Semites as foreshadowing the Nazi solution to the problem of Judaism. But if, among possible rereadings of Luther, one can choose between a Luther of the left, revolutionary and internationalist, and a Luther of the right, the voice of the soil and the blood, the ancestor of national-socialism, it is presumably because both perspectives have falsified the picture. One interprets Luther through one's own colored glasses.

POPULAR IMPACT

Yet undoubtedly Luther had a tremendous impact on his world. One should try to assess this impact with objectivity and sobriety. There was first the popular impact of his writings and his actions. That the Ninety-five Theses gained an immense popularity in a very short time is acknowledged by all historians; Luther lived at the right time. His supporters were from all classes and walks of life, and his influence upon them was equal to their enthusiasm about him. This is not to say, however, that Luther always did what he wanted with his followers. In fact, he had to struggle with dogged determination at many points in his career. In particular, in the lands that became Lutheran, the transformation of the clergy from Mass-saying priests to preachers of the Word was not an easy step. Moreover, the nobility that supported Luther was not entirely motivated by zeal for the gospel; the seizure of monasteries and their lands was an attractive proposition to princes who were beset by recurring financial problems. It is more at the level of religious education that Luther's influence on the people was widespread and lasting. His two catechisms (with their divisions into the Decalogue, the Creed, the Lord's Prayer, and the sacraments) became the basic tools for teaching Lutherans. But they also were the models for most catechisms in other parts of Christendom. Calvin adopted their structure for some of his early works on which his later *Institutes of the Christian Religion* was based. And in 1565 the *Catechism of the Council of Trent* came into being in order to provide an instrument of Catholic education that would do what catechisms were doing in Protestant areas. It even keeps Luther's structure, though in another order (the Creed, the sacraments, the Decalogue, the Lord's Prayer). All Catholic catechisms until the present generation have been modeled on it.

Through his translation of the Bible Luther contributed to the evolution of the German language. The kind of German into which he rendered the Old and the New Testaments became, thanks to the spread of his translation, the model for the modern "high German" which is the standard form of the language today. First popularized in the Lutheran and Reformed parts of Germany, this type of German spread through the Catholic areas during the course of the eighteenth century. As a result Luther's personal impact on German literature has been immeasurable.

In the area of doctrine Luther is of course the chief teacher for what became the Lutheran churches, although Lutheranism incorporated in its confessional books, along with some writings by Luther (the two catechisms, the *Smalcald Articles*), writings by Melanchthon (the *Augsburg Confession* and its *Apology*, the *Treatise on the Power and Primacy of the Pope*), and the agreement called the *Formula of Concord*. His influence on Melanchthon, the ablest theologian among his immediate followers, was very great. It was Luther's conception of the personal dimension of faith and redemption that Melanchthon selected as the focus of his *Loci communes* (1521), the first systematic theology composed in Luther's camp. Furthermore, Melanchthon explained and defended Luther's theology as a whole in the *Augsburg Confession* (1530) and the *Apology* (1531). Yet Melanchthon did not simply follow Luther. He also had ideas of his own, as when he eliminated the incarnation and the Trinity from the *Loci communes* with the suggestion that these should be believed but not made the object of theological speculation. More dramatically, Melanchthon himself was one of the first to try to modify Luther's theology in order to extend a hand of fellowship in the direction of Calvinism. For this purpose he rewrote the text of the *Augsburg Confession* in what is called the *variata* edition (1540). The controversies between Melanchthon's followers and his opponents, the gnesio-Lutherans, that followed the death of Luther led to the agreement embodied in the *Formula of Concord* (1577). This represented a victory for strict Lutheranism; yet it also marked the beginning of the movement that was to couch Luther's thoughts in those scholastic categories that he had rejected.

While Luther's influence continued among his followers both through the reprinting of his works and through the reformulation of his thoughts, it also spread to other areas of the Christian world. John Calvin, the French reformer of Geneva, considered himself a follower of Luther and made some of Luther's ideas, such as justification by faith alone, central to his theological synthesis. This synthesis took shape progressively in the successive editions of the *Institutes of the Christian Religion.* Yet the author's own originality dominates the system as a whole, and Calvin follows his own lead in matters of sacraments and church organization.

Both directly and through Calvinism Luther was influential in the English Reformation. The Thirty-nine Articles (1562), chiefly composed by Archbishop Cranmer, incorporated some basic conceptions of Luther's—among others, Scripture alone (article 6), the bondage of the will (article 10), justification by faith alone (article 11), predestination (article 17), and purgatory (article 22), though the articles on sacraments are more largely influenced by Calvin. Generally speaking, however, the Elizabethan settlement followed a path of its own, for it kept large doses of Catholicism, especially in its liturgy (the *Book of Common Prayer* of 1549 and of 1552, the latter more Protestant than the former) and in the episcopal organization of the church. In their systematic theologies, however, some great theologians of the Elizabethan settlement, such as Richard Hooker, understood righteousness to be based on the pattern of double righteousness, one from Christ and one from the believer, rather than according to Luther's formulation. Although Luther occasionally did use the imagery of double and even triple righteousness, he roundly rejected the doctrine of twofold righteousness when this became the basis for a compromise between some of his followers (including Melanchthon) and some Catholic delegates at the colloquy of Regensburg (1541). Unlike the standard Anglicans, the Puritans were more influenced by the Calvinism of Scotland (John Knox) than by Luther on the matter of justification in particular and in their theology in general.

In the later history of the Reformation there were occasional revivals of some of Luther's emphases. By reacting to what seemed to be the dry speculative theology of Lutheran Orthodoxy, pietism in Germany and Moravia (Count Zinzendorf) restored the warmer aspects of Luther's piety. Through the Moravian brethren Luther's understanding of justification by faith was instrumental in the early stages of the Methodist movement. It was in 1738 when he listened to an explanation of justification by faith that John Wesley "felt his heart strangely warmed." Wesley, however, was led little by little to react against the doctrine of the bound will. Repelled by the Calvinist notion of double predestination (as endorsed at the Synod of Dortrecht in 1619), Wesley also rejected Luther's commentary on Galatians when he read it in 1741. Though he still endorsed justification by faith, the founder of Methodism modified it considerably through his understanding of the human will's cooperation with grace, his teaching that there are several degrees of faith, his emphasis on law, and his belief that it is possible to "go on to perfection" here on earth.

INFLUENCE ON CATHOLIC THEOLOGY

Luther also had an influence in his own time upon some trends in Catholic theology, notably on the advocates of reform that some historians call the Catholic evangelicals. These were men and women who generally shared Luther's doctrine of justification by faith alone and his insistence on Scripture alone as the standard of faith. But they never formed a consistent group, and eventually they either went over to the Reformation or became marginal Catholics. More important, however, for the Catholic church as a whole was Luther's direct and indirect influence on the reforming Council of Trent (1545–1563). Admittedly, Luther sharply denounced the council in the last years of his life. And indeed some of the strictures of the council against the Reformation were aimed at Luther and Lutheranism. But the influence of Luther and of the Council of Trent cannot be properly assessed by paying attention only to their anathemas. It is necessary to go beyond the polemical formulas and perceive the intent of each doctrinal affirmation.

To a great extent the agenda of the Council of Trent was set by the reformers. The council's task was to bring reform to what needed it, and to answer the reformers' doctrinal critique. It is necessary to pay attention to the reformers in order even to understand the structure of the council. And although some sessions seem to have had in mind the Calvinist rather than the Lutheran wing of the Reformation, it was

Luther's figure that loomed in the background of the 25 sessions of the council.

Luther had asked for a council that would base its decisions on Scripture alone. And therefore the first order of business, after the preliminary sessions, was to describe the basis of the Catholic faith. Session three affirmed its allegiance to the Nicene Creed (which of course Luther fully shared); session four declared its fidelity to "the purity of the gospel" as contained in both Scripture and the apostolic traditions. Divergences have appeared among Catholic scholars in interpreting this decree. Yet it is generally accepted today that the division of Scripture and tradition into two distinct and partial sources of revelation is neither taught nor rejected by Trent; such a division only comes from later interpreters.

Though standing closer than Luther to the humanism of the Renaissance, Trent devoted no decree to the question of free will. Instead, its session four examined the question of original sin which lay at the source of Luther's view of the bondage of the will. The decree is directed against neo-Pelagians (who water down the gravity of original sin as transmitted to all humankind) and Anabaptists (who reject infant baptism). One of Luther's main concerns, the exact impact of original sin on the capacities of reason and the will, is not examined, presumably because there were differences on this point between the Thomists, Scotists, and Nominalists, the main schools of theology represented at the council. Luther's old-fashioned Augustinian language, which called concupiscence sin (whereas for Scholasticism as for Trent it is only the result of sin), is explicitly rejected.

Justification, the central point in Luther's theology, is treated at length in session four. Here the council does not use Luther's language, yet the bishops presumably thought that some of the thirty-three anathemas appended to the sixteen chapters of the decree condemned some points of Luther's language and doctrine. But it is debatable how well the bishops were themselves acquainted with the exact meaning of the doctrines of the reformer. One can certainly propose an interpretation of the doctrine of Trent on justification that fully endorses the notions of merit, of preparation for and cooperation with grace, and of sanctification as a process which, starting from justification, leads the faithful to the highest degrees of holiness. Yet the conciliar texts are also compatible with a view that so stresses the centrality of faith that the differences with Luther are more verbal than real. Indeed, Trent repeated the standard scholastic teaching that the only faith that justifies is the one that has been "informed," or animated, by love. In Trent as in most of medieval theology, love is not a work that follows faith, flowing as it were from it; it is an infused gift, entirely due to God, bestowed together with faith and hope and enabling the receiver to respond to God's call in loving God and neighbor. In other words, Trent attempted to effect a synthesis between the Augustinian doctrine of grace as reflected in the main schools of medieval theology and the nearly exclusive concern for faith which Luther had adopted. The formulas are not Luther's, but the exact difference between them is a moot point.

In keeping with the attention paid by Luther to the sacraments, the remaining doctrinal sessions of Trent deal chiefly with sacramental questions. The sacraments are looked at first in general and then in particular. Special attention is paid to the Eucharist. Here Trent opposes Luther. It maintains the seven sacraments. It affirms the eucharistic presence and defends the doctrine of transubstantiation as an expression of the real presence. It also defends the idea that the Eucharist can be truly called a sacrifice, though not a new one, and that as a sacrifice the Mass may be offered for the living and for the dead. In all this, however, there is no allusion to the basis of Luther's sacramental theology, which tied sacrament in the strict sense to the promise of justification. At Trent the notion of sacraments is broader. Under these conditions it seems probable that the council fathers and theologians were not aware of Luther's exact stance. It is therefore debatable what they would have said of the number of sacraments if they had adopted Luther's stricter definition.

The final decree examines the problem which had been the start of Luther's reforming career: indulgences. The same final session treats briefly of purgatory, the invocation of saints, holy pictures, and the relics of saints. These are the most un-Lutheran of the conciliar decrees. At first sight the council would seem to promote those practices to which Luther had objected. Yet it also invites the faithful to moderation in all such matters; it tells the bishops that all must be done with a view to edification. Decrees on these topics probably would have had a very different tone had not Luther protested against abuses he had witnessed.

There may be different views of Luther's real impact on the Council of Trent and on the Counter-Reformation. Yet one can argue that the transformation of Catholic theology from the Middle Ages to modern times was due primarily to Luther's dominant influence on the evolution of European thought. The Scholasticism of the Counter-Reformation was anti-Lutheran and anti-Calvinistic, whereas both Lutheranism and Calvinism developed their own types of scholastic theology. In its attempt at renewal using the thought of Thomas Aquinas, the neo-Scholasticism of the late nineteenth century largely ignored Luther. But toward the middle of the nineteenth century, modern Catholic theology partly developed from the encounter in the Tübingen school between German Catholic theologians and the thought of Luther and Lutheranism.

CONTEMPORARY PHILOSOPHY

By and large modern thinking is not theological. Yet it is significant for Luther's central position in the history of Western civilization that some contemporary philosophical trends are particularly indebted to Luther, whether they acknowledge it or not. We have already mentioned the origins of Marxism in Hegel's dialectic, which itself arose against the background of Luther's sense of time and process. The Enlightenment and its liberal philosophies generally owe more to the followers of Calvin and Zwingli than to those of Luther. But the movement marked by Immanuel Kant could be interpreted as the secularizing of some of Luther's ideas. Luther's dichotomy between faith alone and the whore reason is reversed in favor of reason alone ("pure reason"). Since the idea of God is classified among the transcendentals unattainable by reason, there is room for faith because it is a purely subjective, a priori presupposition of piety. For Luther ethics is the theater of the tragic, in which one struggles with forces beyond oneself, those of evil as well as those of the Spirit. For Kant ethics has been robbed of its mystery; it simply belongs to the will, which is the free agent of moral action in obedience to a "categorical imperative," itself merely humanistic. In the meantime Luther's basic thrust has been singularly distorted.

Some nineteenth-century philosophers, such as Schopenhauer and above all Nietzsche, retrieved the sense of the tragic. But Schopenhauer turned to Buddhism for inspiration while Nietzsche explicitly excluded the Christian dimension, without which none of Luther's stresses and insights make any sense.

Thanks to the Danish Lutheran thinker, Søren Kierkegaard, the authentic Luther has had a more direct impact on contemporary philosophy. Kierkegaard is the founder of modern existentialism. With him, however, this is not yet a philosophy but rather a theological reflection on Christianity. Kierkegaard's intention is to bring faith out of the confusion into which it has been thrown by "a disoriented orthodoxy which knew not what it did, and a revolutionary heterodoxy which knew demonically what it did and only to that extent does not know what it does." Affirmation of the "infinitely qualitative difference" between God and creation restores the paradox of faith. The language and perspective are more modern than Luther's. But this modernity leads to a retrieval of Luther's view of the Christian as "just and sinful" and of faith as shattering all human complacency: "Oh, mad inconsiderateness of faith, which out of consideration for the true all has become blind to all considerations!" Because of their indebtedness to Kierkegaard, the more recent existentialist philosophies of Martin Heidegger and Jean-Paul Sartre contain, in spite of their real or practical atheism, echoes of Luther's central affirmation.

Kierkegaard himself was involved in heated polemics (a series published under the general name *Attack on Christendom*) against prominent members of his own church, the Lutheran Church of Denmark, whom he believed unfaithful to the gospel. Yet through attacking the institutionalized Lutheranism of his country, he was in fact criticizing the whole of Christendom. Kierkegaard's denunciation of Christendom as the betrayer of true Christianity was based precisely on his understanding of justification by faith alone. In contrast to esthetic existence on the one hand and ethical existence on the other, faith brings one into an entirely new domain by relying only on a promise. It demands a leap into an abyss, which is that of the cross. But both the promise and the cross belong to Christ. And it is in Christ's words and deeds that faith is grounded.

In Kierkegaard as in Luther one feels the reforming edge of the principle of justification by faith. It is not as a point of departure for systematic theology that this principle has been the most fruitful. In fact, systems built upon it from the sixteenth century to the nineteenth have tended to blur the principle, to domesticate it. Luther himself never used it for doing systematic theology. It is a reforming principle, for it serves to pinpoint those elements that constantly weaken the originality and the power of the Christian message. In its light the church and the churches can still hear the call to reform in accordance with the gospel.

The great reforming moment of our time has been the Second Vatican Council. In addition to the rediscovery of the historical Luther by Catholic as well as Lutheran and other scholars, the reforms of Vatican II have made it possible for Catholics to take a new look at Luther's doctrinal positions. Admittedly the council itself did not explicitly refer to Luther's testimony. Yet its *Dogmatic Constitution on Divine Revelation,* issued in 1965, highlighted both Scripture and faith in ways which were at least indirectly indebted to Martin Luther. Of Scripture it said: "The study of the sacred text should be so to speak the soul of sacred theology" (n.24); "To ignore the Scriptures is to ignore Christ" (n.25). On faith it affirmed: "To God who reveals himself is due the 'obedience of faith' (Romans 16:26), by which man freely pledges himself to God, giving 'God the full submission of his intelligence and will' . . ." (n.5). The reforming principle is also suggested: the *magisterium* (that is, teaching authority) "is not above God's Word; it rather serves the Word, teaching only what has been transmitted, as, by divine mandate and with the Spirit's assistance, it listens to God's Word with piety, keeps it in awe, and expounds it with fidelity" (n.10). Thus Vatican II began to orient Catholic theology toward reading the works of Luther with greater understanding and to interpret his life and ministry with deeper sympathy.

In addition, the council's openness to ecumenism, its invitation to Lutheran and Protestant as well as Anglican and Orthodox official

observers, the personal relationship that developed between Pope
Paul VI and a Lutheran exegete and theologian, Oscar Cullmann, have
marked a new stage in the development of Catholic thought. Luther
is no longer treated as an adversary. Even though he may still be
viewed critically, he is becoming a source of inspiration to whose
reforming voice Catholic theology needs to listen because it is a voice
from within earlier Catholic tradition. As the doctor of faith, Luther
should rank alongside St. Augustine, the doctor of grace.

SEMIOTIC SQUARE

This brief survey of Luther's influence may well conclude on an un-
familiar note. To a great extent existentialism is already outmoded.
Philosophical moods, unlike the gospel, come and go. A new age has
dawned in science with the explosion of technology and the spread of
micro-computers. A new age has dawned also in philosophy, even
though it may be premature to give it a name. One of its characteristics
is the concern for structures and structural analysis. Out of this has
sprung a new discipline, semiotics (the study of signs and signification).
One of the keys to this science is the "semiotic square," which results
from a reinterpretation of some aspects of the logic of Aristotle. In the
semiotic square a number of contemporary linguists, literary critics,
ethnologists, and anthropologists profess to have found a pathway that
leads into the inner structure of human society, human language, and
even human thought.

The semiotic square already appears in, of all places, Luther's commentary of 1519 on Galatians 5. Taking a clue from Romans 6:6–7,
Luther draws a diagram: "Let us," he writes, "put it in order and
structure:

free from righteousness	slavery to sin
slavery to righteousness	free from sin."

Luther comments: "He who is free from sin is made the slave of
righteousness. He who is the slave of sin is free from righteousness,
and vice versa." This formulation in fact corresponds exactly to the
analysis of meaning in contemporary semiotics. The freedoms of righteousness and of sin stand in reciprocal contradiction, as do the slav-

eries of sin and of righteousness. In the order of righteousness, freedom and slavery imply or presuppose each other just as they do in the
order of sin. The paradox of the Christian condition is that it remains
the human condition, where sin brings slavery through its own kind
of freedom, and yet it is already the condition of the kingdom, where
the righteousness of Christ brings freedom through another kind of
slavery.

With this diagramming of freedom and slavery, Luther already stood
at the frontier of the twenty-first century. Yet what he was saying came
straight from the earliest echoes, in the letters of Paul, of the revelation
of the Word of God in Jesus Christ.

FOR STUDY AND DISCUSSION

1. To what can Luther's great influence in the church and in society be attributed? What are specific developments in the modern world for which Luther is often credited?

2. Assess the popular impact of Luther's writings (especially his catechisms and his translation of the Bible) and his actions. What influence did Luther have also outside of "Lutheranism"?

3. What influence did Luther have on trends in Catholic theology? What were the chief issues discussed at the various sessions of the Council of Trent? What is the doctrine of transubstantiation, and how does this doctrine differ from Luther's view of the Eucharist? Which are the most un-Lutheran decrees of the Council of Trent?

4. What are some contemporary philosophical trends that are indebted to Luther? Who was Søren Kierkegaard, and how has Luther had a direct impact on contemporary philosophy through him?

5. Describe the semiotic square as it appears in Luther's commentary of 1519 on Galatians 5.

6. How can Luther be considered "a reformer for the churches"?

For Further Reading

Burgess, Joseph, and George H. Tavard. *Studies for Lutheran/Catholic Dialogue.* Minneapolis: Augsburg Publishing House, 1980.

Kierkegaard, Søren. *Christian Discourses.* New York and London: Oxford University Press, 1961.

———. *Fear and Trembling.* Garden City, N.Y.: Doubleday & Co., 1954.